THE
UNICORN
Factor™

Demystifying Marketing Content to
Set You Apart From the Crowd

by Regina Andler

Edited by Lil Barcaski

Published by: GWN Publishing
www.GWNPublishing.com

Cover Design: Kristina Conatser

ISBN: 978-1-959608-94-3

Dedication

For Mom and Dad, who always reminded me that words have the power to change the world. I will love you always and forever.

Foreword

I am so thrilled to be able to introduce you to this incredible book, *The Unicorn Factor*, which was authored by Regina Andler, who has been both a friend and a colleague of mine while working as a business consultant and marketing specialist. Since Regina and I have been working together for more than four years, I can confidently say that she is extremely knowledgeable in her field.

Do you agree that it can be challenging to stand out in today's competitive market? Everyone is attempting to attract attention, and it may appear to be impossible to get someone's attention. What would happen, however, if there was a way to glow like a unicorn in the midst of a field of horses and rise above all the noise? That is exactly the subject matter that *The Unicorn Factor* encompasses.

This book provides an in-depth analysis of Regina's exclusive approach to the production of distinctive and original content. Your approach to social media, lead magnets, and video content is going to be fundamentally altered as a result of this book, *The Unicorn Factor*. These are the most important aspects in which you need to excel, in order to pull in and maintain your audience.

One of the things that I really like about this book is how useful it is. The advice that Regina gives you is not general. She walks you through each step of the process for you to follow. You will find real-world examples and straightforward advice that you can immediately put into practice. Regardless of whether you are just beginning your journey or are trying to better your content game, this book contains everything you need.

It is clear that Regina has put all of her expertise and experience into writing this book. Having a deep understanding of the specific issues that coaches and consultants face, she has developed solutions that are shown to be effective. I have personal experience with the ways in which her strategies can completely revolutionize a company, and I am confident that they can do the same for you.

As you navigate through *The Unicorn Factor*, you should prepare to perceive the content you use for marketing in a completely different light. You will witness an increase in your engagement as well as the growth of your business if you follow Regina's suggestions. When it comes to distinguishing out and achieving success, this book is more than simply a handbook; it is your ticket.

When it comes to marketing material, you should get ready to demystify it and differentiate yourself from the competition.

Get reading and implement what you learn.

Terri Levine, Marketing Consultant, Bestselling Author of *The Conversion Equation*

www.heartrepreneur.com

Table of Contents

The Unicorn Factor™ — An Introduction 1

SECTION 1: Your Unique Business 5

SECTION 2: Your Unique Audience 21

SECTION 3: Your Unique Story 33

SECTION 4: Your Unique Content 41

SECTION 5: Your Unicorn Factor 113

Useful Resources 125

Acknowledgments. 131

About the Author 133

The Unicorn Factor™ — An Introduction

There are different types of horses in the world. There are work horses, thoroughbreds, ponies and more. The unicorn, however, is a creature, with mystical qualities that make it unique.

But a unicorn without a horn is just another horse.

It is that magical horn that sets the unicorn apart from the rest of the herd.

In 2002, when I started my first business, I was just like one of those common horses. I took course after course learning how to set up my sales and marketing to bring in new clients. I followed the herd and learned how to do sales and marketing the "traditional" way, and it was not a cheap process!

I learned pitches, closings, marketing funnels and all those so-called proven ways to sell my services; none worked. I worked hard to create marketing content to attract new clients. When I got frustrated because it wasn't working, I met with my business consultant who told me to stick with the process and keep pushing prospects until they bought one of my programs.

The thing was it never felt right. It actually felt kind of dirty.

I learned to hate sales and marketing. Even the mere mention of the words "sales and marketing" had my skin crawling back then. I felt like the stereotypical sleazy car salesman.

Did you ever hear the phrase "follow like a lemming"? A lemming is a little rodent. A group of lemmings will follow the lead lemming anywhere, even off a cliff to their demise. To "follow like a lemming" means to follow blindly, without any thought or regard to the consequences.

That was exactly what I had been doing. I was a lemming, and I was headed for the cliff. They were trying to turn me into someone I didn't want to be. Now don't get me wrong, my business was doing okay, but not great. We were bringing in a solid 6 figures annually, but I knew it could be better. I knew inside that something was not quite right, but I just couldn't put my finger on it.

As a self-proclaimed science geek, I look at all things as energy. Everything is energy. If something does not "feel" right, the energy is not right. Well, this didn't feel right.

All energy has a specific frequency and vibration. In order to be successful, your frequency and vibration must match the energy of whatever it is you are seeking. If you want more money, you must be on the same frequency as money. If you want more clients, you must be on the same frequency as your ideal client. If not, you will forever be chasing the illusive dream. The only way to get what you want is to shift your energy—your frequency and vibration—to match what you want.

It was not until 2020 that I finally fully embraced what I now call my inner unicorn.

I started doing things a little different from what I had been taught. Instead of telling my audience how I was going to help them, I started asking them what they needed. Immediately, I began to like what I was doing again. I felt that I was back on the right path. I had shifted my energy. I stopped using all those cookie-cutter templates that those so-called gurus provided (that everyone else was using, too) and started creating marketing content that I, myself, would act on. I found that the simple change of asking my audience what they needed, and then giving them exactly that, made me stand out from the rest of the crowd. Radical, right?

I began to shift the way I thought about the marketing process. My marketing mindset took a 180-degree turn, and I began to love creating marketing content.

I stopped trying to "sell" people.

I changed all my pitchy-salesy marketing content to that of value-based content and that was exactly what my audience was looking for. The result: *The Unicorn Factor*™ methodology was born.

Does any of this sound familiar to you?

- Do you feel overwhelmed, anxious, and frustrated that your business is not moving as fast as you would like?

- Do you spend most of your day on social media trying to find new clients?

- Do you continuously write new content that no one ever reads?

- Do you see other people in your industry who are making the type of income that you want to make, and you wonder how they're able to do it?

- Are you burning yourself out and wondering why you ever decided to go into business in the first place?

When it comes to attracting new clients in the world today, you must create marketing content that sets you apart from everyone else trying to attract the same audience.

You do that by tapping into your inner unicorn.

Let's face it, no one ever made history by being ordinary. If you have been creating marketing content that no one reads; posts that no one likes, comments or shares; blogs or articles that fall flat; emails that always end up in the junk folder, or any other marketing content that your audience is not connecting with, then you need what is in this book.

When you read *The Unicorn Factor™ — How To Demystify Marketing Content To Set You Apart From The Crowd*, you will learn:

- How to zone in on your ideal client avatar to create unique content that speaks directly to them.
- How to break away from all those cookie-cutter, traditional marketing processes and create a marketing process unique to you and your business.
- How to engage your audience and have them ask how they can work with you instead of you trying to sell them.
- How to use your unique story to showcase your expertise.
- How to spend less time on social media and more time talking to qualified prospects.
- How to stand out from the rest of the crowd.

When you follow *The Unicorn Factor™* methodology, you will attract more of your target audience into your circles, and as a result, you will get new clients.

Are you ready? It's time for you to set yourself apart from the rest of the herd.

It's time to break out your magical horn and let your inner unicorn shine!

YOUR UNIQUE BUSINESS

"To be successful you must be unique, you must be so different that if people want what you have, they must come to you to get it."

—Walt Disney

Why does your business need to be unique and what does that even mean?

In the world today there are millions of entrepreneurs. Take a look at your industry. How many others are in your industry doing what you do? Chances are there are quite a lot…and that's a *GOOD* thing. Building and sustaining a successful business in this day and age requires you to stand out from the rest of the crowd.

The Mindset of Business

I get it. Being one in the massive crowd in your industry can be a bit intimidating. If you are new to business, even more so. Stop right now and think, "Am I freaked out or energized with the idea that there are a lot of others doing what I do?" Most people will say they are freaked out. Whether you are freaked out or energized, understand that business is all about mindset. Once you have your mindset in the right place, success will follow.

Why did you start your business? If you instantly replied, "To make money!", then, I have to tell you, you are in business for the wrong reason. Hear me out for a sec.

Of course, we all want and need money to live in this world today, however, money should not be the reason you went into business; it should be the by-product. If you said you started your business to make money, you are likely dealing with a scarcity mindset.

Let me ask you this. Does any of this sound familiar or strike a nerve?

- You are constantly thinking about what you don't have.
- You are afraid of running out of resources, so you are reluctant to share and / or collaborate with others.
- You believe there is only so much money to go around so you need to get what you can and hold onto it tightly.
- You feel envious or threatened when you see others in your industry succeeding more than you.
- You are afraid of failure or even success, so you often find yourself procrastinating.

If any of those sound familiar to you, then you, my friend, have a scarcity mindset.

But there is good news! Once you recognize it, and own it, you can do something about it. What does this have to do with writing content that makes you stand out from the crowd?

Everything.

All the content you create, whether you realize it or not, reflects your tone, your values, and your mindset. If you have a scarcity mindset around your business, you will never be able to create unique engaging content for your audience. When it comes to your unique business, what makes it unique is *YOU* and it all starts with all that stuff going on in your head. If you do not believe you can be successful, guess what? You won't. If you believe there are too many others out there who have more experience than you out there, guess what? You are correct. There will always be others with more experience. So what?

Your brain is the most powerful tool you have. It can make or break you. It is where all your beliefs are hanging out. And limiting beliefs will hold you back no matter how well you write your content.

Some of the most common limiting beliefs that entrepreneurs have include:

- There is only so much money to go around.
- Money is the root of all evil.
- I'm not good enough to compete with others who have been in the business longer.
- I'm not smart enough.
- I have a fear of failure.

And there are many more. So, before we can even get into creating your unique content, let's squash these limiting beliefs in the bud and open up your mind to let your unique creativity flow.

Most people walk around life without even considering that they are the ones in control of their minds. Left to its own devices, your subconscious mind creates your reality, and it will come up with all kinds of reasons for you to fail. It will create false stories based on information it has accumulated throughout your lifetime. It will keep you stuck on a hamster wheel making the same mistakes over and over again.

Are you going to let your subconscious mind run wild and free and out of control?

Your brain is *YOUR* brain. Are you going to let it come up with all kinds of crazy notions about how your life should be" Or are you going to grab the reins and take control? It is time to shift control back over to your conscious mind and get rid of those old, stale limiting beliefs. I just happen to have a very simple process for removing these limiting beliefs; I call it the *A.I.R.* method.

The first thing to understand is that any limiting belief you have has been hanging out in your brain for quite some time and is not going to disappear overnight.

The key is in the first step of the A.I.R. method which is to *Acknowledge* that you have a limiting belief. Simply bring the belief into your conscious mind so that you can start working on it.

Acknowledge potential limiting beliefs. **(List your beliefs below.)**

> EXAMPLE: *"I'm not smart enough." "There are not enough clients to go around." "What if no one wants what I have to offer?" etc.*

1. _____

_____

_____

_____

_____

2. _____

_____

_____

_____

3. _____

_____

_____

_____

Congratulations on acknowledging that you have a limiting belief that is holding you back! Now it is time to *Identify* the truth about the belief. Why do you believe it? Is it even true?

Identify why you believe it. **(Write down where your limiting belief came from.)**

> EXAMPLE: *Belief: "I'm not smart enough." Ask yourself, IS THAT TRUE?*

> TIP: If you say to yourself, "Yes, it is true because…" The key to squashing that belief lies in your "because." Take a good hard look at whatever came after the "because." Pretend you are a three-year-old and keep asking yourself "Why?" until you get to the root of the belief.

1. _____

_____

_____

_____

2. _____

_____

_____

3. _____

_____

_____

We all have limiting beliefs that we believe to be true, and yet when we sit with them for a moment and really think it out, we find that maybe it used to be true a long time ago, but not so much now. Or maybe it was never true. Maybe it was someone else's belief. Maybe a belief one of your parents had.

Congratulations! You just completed a major step in removing a limiting belief by identifying where it originated and recognizing that it is no longer true or maybe it was never true!

Now it is time to *Replace* the old belief with a new belief. What is true for you now?

Replace your old belief with a new belief that better serves the person you are today. (**Write out your NEW belief.**)

> EXAMPLE: *Old belief: "I'm not smart enough." New belief: "I have had years of training in this field. I have years of experience where I lived through what I now teach others, so they do not have to make the same mistakes I made. I am very knowledgeable in my field!*

1.

2.

3.

One important thing to remember is that limiting beliefs will pop up over and over again in your brain until you have completely replaced them with a new, more empowering belief. The key is to catch them fast before they wreak havoc on your mindset.

Be mindful of the thoughts going through your head, especially when things are not going quite as well as you would like. Stop and consider what triggered the thought and then ask yourself, "Is it true?" Repeat the A.I.R. exercise any time you feel a limiting belief surfacing.

Remember, we all have limiting beliefs. The goal is to make sure they do not stop you from creating your unique content and building your successful business.

Your Unique Purpose Statement

Now that your head is in the right place, let me ask you again, why did you start your business? At the core of every business owner is a driving force that keeps them going in good times and bad. When was the last time you sat down and really thought about your core purpose? Before you can create unique, authentic content that will engage your audience, you need to be crystal clear on why you are doing what you are doing.

You need to create your **Unique Purpose Statement.**

Your energy is reflected in your content, whether written or spoken. If you have ever sat through a long, drawn-out presentation where the speaker had a monotone voice that just seemed to drone on and on until you literally wanted to scream, you know what I mean. Conversely, if you have ever listened to a speaker who had you at the edge of your seat listening intently throughout the entire presentation, it's the same thing. It is all energy.

The boring presenter likely does not have any real reason for doing what they are doing other than a paycheck. There is no passion in their presentation. No energy.

The riveting presenter's passion is coming through in every word they speak. Their energy is so infectious that even if it is a boring topic, you are still interested in what they have to say.

Your written content works the same way. It reflects your tone. Are you creating monotone, boring content or unique, interesting content that engages your audience and has them hanging on to every word?

When you do not have a clear purpose and a powerful reason for doing what you do, your content is likely pretty monotone and boring. Your Unique Purpose Statement is the core of why you do what you do. The "unique" part is the part of your statement that sets you apart from others in your space.

Here are a few real-life examples of Unique Purpose Statements as examples.

> *"My purpose is to leave as many situations as possible, every day, even in small ways, better than I find them. I enjoy doing this as a Keynote Speaker, Visualization Coach, Creator of the Vision Board Mastery learning program and co-founder of a 501c3 called Beachbum Philanthropy."* STEVE GAMLIN, THE MOTIVATIONAL FIREWOOD® GUY

> *"My purpose is to Ignite Joy in the world around me. I am privileged to do that by helping midlife professional women create joy through change with my proprietary Heart Compass Method™"* VELMA GALLANT, HEART-SET ADVISOR, COMPASS INTERCONNECT.

> *"My unique purpose is to be super present in whatever moment or circumstance I find myself. This heightened presence allows me to serve others while at the same time serving myself. It allows me to see, hear, feel, taste and touch beyond the physical & recognize the greatness in each and every soul I come across. I aim to bring a sense of "Joy" to the world for those that may feel it no longer exists. When someone walks away from*

me feeling better about themselves and the world after our inter-action, then I have accomplished my purpose." KEN ATTARD, MINDSET MALTA

"My purpose is to positively impact as many lives as I can throughout my lifetime and leave a ripple effect that continues long after I am gone. I do this by using my lifetime of knowl-edge and skills to empower and inspire coaches and consul-tants to build successful lifestyle businesses and through my philanthropic pursuits." REGINA ANDLER, AUTUMN ASCENT CONSULTING LLC

Take some time to reflect on why you do what you do. Write out your **Unique Purpose Statement**. Reflect on these questions to gain clarity on your purpose.

1. Which activities make you lose track of time? What topics do you find yourself constantly researching or discussing with enthusiasm?

2. What do you stand for? What principles guide your decisions and actions? Make a list of your core values and prioritize them based on their significance to you.

3. How have your life experiences shaped your beliefs, values, and outlook on life?

4. What are you naturally good at? What skills have you devel-oped through education, training, or experience?

5. What is the impact you want to make on the world?

Once you have considered all of these questions, connect the dots, and write out your Unique Purpose Statement. Share it with some trusted friends and get their feedback. They may help you add a few things you didn't even think of.

Knowing your Unique Purpose Statement will help you create greater impact with your content.

Unique Purpose Statement

_____

_____

_____

_____

_____

_____

_____

_____

_____

_____

_____

_____

_____

_____

Your Core Genius

As you build and scale your business, your ultimate goal should be working in your core genius every day. Your core genius refers to your innate talents, skills and strengths that are unique to you. It's what drives your purpose. It *is* your Unicorn Factor.

Are you a health coach, a business consultant, a speaker coach, a life coach, an executive coach, or a relationship coach? There are thousands of different types of coaches and consultants in just about every industry today. Where do you fit in? When you define your core genius, you know exactly what you should be focusing on and what you should be delegating to others. Knowing your core genius also builds your confidence and further helps you squash any of those lingering limiting beliefs.

What skills and resources do you bring to the table?

My favorite tool for identifying core genius is a mind map. Here are the steps for zeroing in on your core genius:

1. On page 19, or on a separate sheet of paper, draw an oval in the middle of the page. Write "My Core Genius" in the oval.

2. Draw a few lines out from the center oval (you can add more if you need them later).

3. On each line, write down one of your skills. Your skill could come from formal training or from personal experience.

4. Continue to create new lines until you can no longer think of additional skills.

5. IMPORTANT STEP: Leave it alone for a day or two. As soon as you start creating the mind map, your subconscious goes into high gear thinking of other skills to add to the list. Go back to your mind map and add those additional skills that come to mind.

6. Go around your mind map and put your finger on one of the lines. Read the line out loud. Pay attention to how you feel (your energy). When you read the skill on the line, does it feel good or not? If it feels good and excites you, circle it. If not, cross it off.

7. Once you have gone around all of the skills and circled or crossed them off, it is time to connect the dots. Of the ones

that are circled, what do they have in common? Reflect on the connection to discover your true core genius.

As you build your unique business, having a mindset for success, knowing your unique purpose and your core genius will set you on track for creating that unique content that will attract your ideal client.

Speaking of your ideal client, who is that? it is time to move on and discover Your Unique Audience.

My Core Genius

THE UNICORN FACTOR

YOUR UNIQUE AUDIENCE

"Great marketing means knowing your audience, talking to your target personas, and building your content strategy around them."

—Rocío Arrarte

Let's get one thing out on the table right now...*EVERYONE* is NOT your client.

Even if what you have can help just about everyone, that does not mean they want or need what you have. You must understand who your unique audience is before you write one word of content.

Your Unique Audience

According to WorldOMeters, there are over 8 billion people in the world today.[1] Chances are pretty good that there are some folks out there who need what you offer, the way you offer it.

---

1   https://www.worldometers.info/world-population/

I get it, you are super passionate about what you do, and you want to help as many people as you can by sharing your knowledge. You may even believe so strongly in your product or service that you believe everyone should invest in it. But… "Everyone" is not a market segment. The cold truth is that 8 billion plus people do not want or need what you sell. You need to identify your unique audience. This is the group of people you will create your content for. This group is a subset of the industry you work in.

Take the wellness industry for example. According to Allied Market Research, the market size of this industry is expected to reach USD \$12.9 trillion (YES! That was with a 'T'!) by 2031.[2] This industry is broken down into many segments. Each of those segments is further broken down into smaller and smaller niches.

Case story:

Many years ago, I was part of a referral networking group that met weekly. At every meeting we each had 1 minute to tell the group about our business and ask for a referral. Week after week I listened to a woman who sold a skincare line get up and say, "… And a good referral for me this week is anyone with skin!" Every week she left disappointed that she received no referrals.

As part of this group, we would meet one-to-one in order to get to know the other person's business better. The objective, to them find qualified referrals.

I met with this woman one day and she told me she was thinking about leaving the group because she not getting any referrals. I asked her if she was open to a suggestion, and she said yes.

I said, "Is there one specific part of your skincare line that stands out from the rest?" She enthusiastically replied, "Yes! Our adult acne line is amazing!" I said, "Great! Next week when you do

---

2   *https://www.alliedmarketresearch.com/ health-and-wellness-market-A29258*

your 1 minute, tell the group a little about this product line and how amazing it is. When it comes time to ask for the referral, tell them that you are specifically looking for women over the age of 40 who are suffering from adult acne." She agreed she would do this.

At the next meeting, She got up and went through her 1 minute as we discussed. When she left the room, she had 3 referrals in hand!

When you get specific, a clear visual is created in the mind of your audience. They know exactly what you do and who you are looking to work with.

Where do you and your products and services fit in? Use the following exercise to get clear on your unique audience.

Step 1: On the following page or on a separate piece of paper, write down and answer each of the following questions.

> PRO TIP: Use a timer and set it for 2 minutes. For each question, write down as many responses as you can think of until the timer goes off.

- QUESTION #1: Who can you help? (It's *NOT* everybody!)
- QUESTION #2: Who do you like to help? Think about past and existing clients.
- QUESTION #3: Who has the money to hire you or buy your products?
- QUESTION #4: Why would they hire you?

1. Who can you help? (It's NOT everybody!)

2. Who do you like to help? Think about past and existing clients.

3. Who has the money to hire you or buy your products?

4. Why would they hire you?

Step 2: Review your list.

Is there a theme where the same response showed up in more than one area? Highlight all of the responses that really resonate with you.

Step 3: Scrub your list.

- Are there any types of clients that you highlighted that you are not qualified to help?

- Are any of the segments identified still too big? For example: "I help business owners get more clients". "Business owners" is a really large segment. Narrow it down to a specific type of business, a narrower niche market, such as, "I help *life coaches* who are just starting their businesses." Or "I help *women* who are *looking to transition out of corporate world* and start their own coaching business."

Step 4: Further narrow down your audience by asking yourself these questions:

1. Am I credible in this segment or can I quickly become credible? If not, you will be spending your time trying to convince people why they need to work with you, and we don't want that.

2. Are there enough people in this segment to build my business from? If not, you may need to reconsider who you can help or widen the segment.

3. Do people in this segment tend to look for help? If not, remove it. Do not waste your time trying to convince someone why they need your product or service.

4. How easy is it for me to reach the people in this segment? Are there organizations, associations, newspapers, mailing lists, social media groups, etc., for this segment?

5. Do people in this segment have the money to purchase my products or services? Don't waste time and money marketing to people who cannot or will not invest in themselves.

6. Are people in this segment the decision makers? If not, you are spending time and money addressing the wrong audience.

At this point, you should have a pretty narrow segment. For example:

- A health coach who specializes in helping people with diabetes reclaim their health.

- A business consultant who works with personal trainers who only provide online training services.

- A skin care specialist who works with post-menopausal women.

Why do you narrow your niche down so small when you know you can serve others? Two words…

MARKETING CONTENT.

If you try to speak to a larger audience, your message will be watered down, less people will see it and engage with it. In the case of content…bigger is definitely not better! Don't worry. Even though you have narrowed the audience, there will be others outside that group who are attracted to what you offer.

The key is to narrow it down enough so you still have a large enough audience to build your business but also narrow enough so you can create unique, targeted content that will attract them. Remember this phrase … "When you speak to *everyone* you speak to *no one.*"

Your Ideal Client Avatar

Now that you know your unique audience, it is time to get down to the nitty gritty of that one single individual in that audience, your ideal client avatar (ICA). Why do you want to get this specific? Because when you begin writing your unique content, you will specifically be speaking to this person and this person only.

With content, consistency is key and if you are all over the place with your marketing topics, you will confuse your audience. And as the saying goes, a confused mind does nothing. When you have a clear understanding of your ideal client avatar, you can develop content that speaks directly to them and provides them with the exact results they are looking for.

Let's get one more thing out on the table: your prospects do not care about you. Seriously. They don't care how many years you have been doing what you are doing. They don't care about your certifications, degrees, or experience. All they care about is...

"CAN YOU PROVIDE THE RESULT I AM LOOKING FOR?"

Humans buy based on emotion and emotion only. From a psychological standpoint, no one buys anything because they want or need it. They buy it because they want the feelings having it will give them.

In a *Psychology Today* blog, Peter Noel Murray Ph.D. notes, "An understanding of consumer purchase behavior must be based on knowledge of human emotion and include the paramount influence that emotions have on decision-making."[3]

---

3   *https://www.psychologytoday.com/us/ blog/inside-the-consumer-mind/201302/ how-emotions-influence-what-we-buy*

CONSIDER THIS: You need to buy a lawn mower because your grass is getting too high. The question is, who cares if it is too high? So what? The thing is, when it gets too high, it bugs you. You don't like looking at that tall grass. You think it makes your yard look like a mess. Inside that makes you feel anxious, maybe even angry that the lawn has got so out of control. You buy a lawn mower so you can cut the lawn. Now, there you are, sitting on your front porch, looking over your perfectly coifed lawn, *feeling* calmer, happier. Get it?

This concept applies to everything we buy. When you tap into your target audience's emotions with your content, you will have their rapt attention and they will be hanging on to every word.

You will never have to "sell" anything. Your ideal clients will be standing in line waiting to join your program or purchase your products. Why? Because they *feel* you can give them the exact results they are looking for. All you need to do is simply extend your hand and offer the solution that they already know they want.

Now, you may say confidently that you already know your ideal client avatar. But I challenge you to revisit that assumption. Why? To make sure you have drilled down deep enough so you can create exceptional content that connects with your audience down to their core.

Here are the main characteristics to define:

1. DEMOGRAPHICS — Gender, age, marital status, income, location, etc. Remember, the narrower the better. For example, instead of an age group between 25 and 65, narrow it down to a closer one, like 45-65.

2. PSYCHOGRAPHICS — Lifestyle, interests, values, beliefs, what they think and feel, etc.

3. WANTS AND NEEDS — Do they have a desire to lose weight? Find more clients? Create stronger relationships? Resolve a health issue? Are they looking for accountability?

4. PAIN POINTS AND FRUSTRATIONS — What are their real or imagined problems? What keeps them up at night? What objectives are they looking to meet? What challenges are they facing?

5. WHERE DO THEY HANG OUT? — Do they seek out help online? By referral? Do they go to networking groups looking for help?

6. WHAT TYPE OF HELP ARE THEY LOOKING FOR? — Are they looking for structured programs? One-to-one consulting? Group consulting? Done-with-you services? Done-for-you services? etc.

Get deep. Once you have all characteristics down, define and describe one single ideal client avatar in such a way that you can see this person in your mind's eye. Give them a name. Find a visual that represents that exact person and tape it someplace where you will see it every day.

Wellness Consultant Ideal Client Avatar Example:

Sarah is a 42-year-old successful businesswoman and a devoted mother living in a suburban area. She leads a busy life, juggling her demanding career as a marketing executive with the responsibilities of raising two children.

Despite her achievements, Sarah often finds herself feeling overwhelmed and stressed, desperately seeking a way to regain balance and improve her well-being.

The overwhelming stress from her busy schedule leaves her feeling emotionally drained. She constantly battles fatigue and struggles to maintain healthy habits.

As a college-educated professional, Sarah is open-minded and curious, willing to explore alternative approaches to wellness beyond traditional medicine.

What Sarah truly desires is a holistic wellness solution that encompasses all aspects of her well-being. She longs for effective stress reduction techniques to manage the pressures of her fast-paced life.

Sarah is tired of constantly feeling drained and is looking for strategies to boost her energy and vitality, allowing her to meet the demands of her career and family with enthusiasm.

She is a health-conscious individual who understands the importance of taking care of herself.

She is proactive, self-motivated, and always looking for ways to enhance her physical and mental health. However, finding time for self-care is a constant struggle, and she yearns for guidance on integrating wellness practices seamlessly into her daily routine.

Sarah is on a journey of personal growth and self-improvement. She understands the importance of self-reflection and is eager to develop a growth-oriented mindset.

She is looking for tools and techniques that will contribute to her overall personal growth.

Above all, Sarah yearns for a better work-life balance that will prevent burnout and find fulfillment in both her career and personal life.

She is ready, willing, and able to hire the right wellness consultant to help her reach her wellness goals.

When you have a crystal-clear understanding of your ideal client avatar, you will be able to create content that is more relevant and engaging. This helps you increase the chances of attracting, connecting with, and converting potential clients.

One last note... this process is iterative and requires continuous monitoring and adaptation. Your niche and ideal client avatar will shift and change as the world shifts and your business grows. Make it a point to review your audience at least once a year to make sure you are still on target.

THE UNICORN FACTOR

YOUR UNIQUE STORY

"When you stand and share your story in an empowering way, your story will heal you and your story will heal somebody else."

—Iyanla Vanzant

The single most powerful tool in your business toolbox is your story. Are you using it to your advantage?

Your Greatest Superpower

Everyone has a story. Sometimes that story is fraught with a lot of challenges, pain, and heartache. *BUT* ... that is exactly what makes YOU unique.

What is your story? We all have one. Chances are pretty good that you are doing what you do today because of what you experienced along your own personal journey. Maybe you have had years of corporate business experience in a particular field and now you are an expert helping others in that field. Maybe some major traumatic event in your life occurred, such as a significant health issue or accident, where you had to endure. Along the way you found ways to get your life back in a place of peace and harmony, and created a step-by-step process to help others do the same.

Whatever your story, whatever the journey, along the way at some point you had a turning point where you realized you could help others facing similar challenges make their journey easier. Your story is your greatest superpower when it comes to your unique content. It is the key to creating a real connection with your audience.

Here are a few reasons why your story is important to share:

1. It builds trust and lets your audience know you are an actual person and not some artificial bot creating content. (Believe me, there are a lot of bots out there today!) Sharing your personal journey, struggles, and successes makes you relatable. It shows that you're not just selling something, but you're someone who's experienced something similar to theirs and overcame those challenges.

2. It separates you from others in your industry. Your story is uniquely yours. In a saturated industry, how you share your personal story can set you apart and make you memorable.

3. Your story engages your audience. Stories captivate people. A well-told personal story will engage your audience more effectively than generic marketing content.

4. Sharing your journey and experiences highlights your skills, knowledge, and experiences. It lets your audience know you have been there, done that, and can help them navigate their journey as well.

5. It creates an emotional connection with others. Sharing your highs and lows lets your audience know that you, too, are human and have gone through experiences that may be very similar to what they are going through right now. Creating an emotional bond with your audience builds trust and helps your audience really connect with you.

Check out these powerful stories from a couple of amazing people.

Hal Elrod[4] is an author, international speaker, and podcaster. He tells his story in his book "The Miracle Morning" about how he died for 6 minutes after a horrific car accident then went on to suffer massive financial troubles where he almost lost his house and everything he had.

His "Miracle Morning" process was born from these life-changing events, and he now has a massive community of followers who have implemented his routine into their day.

Hal's belief is that anyone can achieve their dreams in every area of life, as long as they are willing to shift their way of thinking to help them create their success.

Nick Vujicic[5] was born with no arms and no legs. When he was just 8 years old, he contemplated suicide. At the age of 10 he tried to drown himself.

After his mother showed him a story of a severely disabled man who was thriving, he finally decided he was going to live a full life without his limbs. He learned how to write with the two toes he has, learned how to type on a computer, to throw a tennis ball and many more things that people with limbs take for granted.

This sent him on a mission to help others who have lost hope. Today, he is an international keynote speaker, bestselling author and he teaches a course on how to cultivate resilience in your personal and business endeavors.

---

4   *https://halelrod.com/*

5   *https://nickvujicic.com/*

These are a couple of extreme circumstance examples of stories. I share them with you to point out that no matter what your story is, your story matters.

Types of Stories

When it comes to writing unique content, your story is that one absolute thing that no one else on earth shares with you. It is uniquely yours. Your story includes everything that has happened up until this point in time, and you will continue to add to it for as long as you live.

In *Section Four — Your Unique Content*, we will go into more detail about how to use your story to your advantage. For now, let's review a few different types of story categories.

The Origin Story

In this type of story, you share how you started your journey in your industry. What inspired you to begin? It is the who, what, where, why, and how you are doing what you do today.

The Turing Point Story

These stories tell of those pivotal moments in your life or business when something significant happened. What were the key decisions you made in order to move forward? Was there an event that set you on a new path?

The Overcoming Obstacles Story

We all face obstacles in our life both personal and professional. Obstacle stories are where you explain the obstacles you faced throughout your journey and the steps you took to overcome them.

The Success Story

Success stories highlight your biggest wins. The exact same wins that your audience is looking to achieve. What were your major achievements and how did you accomplish them?

The Lessons Learned Story

We all mess up. We all fail from time to time. These stories highlight those moments when things did not go as planned, yet you were able to learn valuable lessons that helped you move forward.

The Behind the Scenes Story

These stories offer a glimpse into your daily life. How do you manage your time? How do you handle stress? What are your daily habits and routines? Giving your audience a look behind the curtain helps create a stronger bond. It shows them your authentic self.

The Community Involvement Story

Community involvement stories give your audience a glimpse of your philanthropic activities. Talking about how you give back to your community and the world helps your followers connect with you on a deeper level.

The Client Success Story

As you work with your clients, capture their story. Client success stories show real-life examples of how you have helped others succeed. Where were they before they started working with you. How did you help them? As a direct result of working with you, where are they now?

These are just some of the many types of story categories you can use based on your personal experience. Sharing these stories in your content will help you connect uniquely and authentically, creating lasting relationships.

Stop right now and take some time to write your story. Grab a sheet of paper and a pen. Think back on who you were before you became the person you are today. Include all the detail, all the challenges, all the struggles. If you don't know where to start, use the following prompts to get you started.

- Identify key moments in your life. They could be significant events, milestones or turning points in your life.

- CREATE A PERSONAL STORY OUTLINE. INCLUDE:
  - Your introduction
  - Your background (where you were before the key moment.)
  - The personal challenges and obstacles that you faced.
  - The turning point. What was that "ah-ha" moment when you decided to make a major shift in your life?
  - Detail your achievements since your shift.
  - What were the lessons learned? Was something specific born from your story, like Hal's *The Miracle Morning* routine?
  - Where are you now?
  - What are your future goals?

A few pointers:

- Remember to be truthful and authentic when telling your story — a.k.a. no fish stories!

- Use descriptive language. Create a narrative that helps your target audience feel what you experienced.

- Be vulnerable. I know, it can be scary putting it all out on the table, but that is exactly what is going to engage your audience.

- Don't get too detailed. Tell your story using the most impact-ful points. Too much detail can dilute your message.

Now that you are clear on your unique business, have a firm grasp on your target audience and ideal client avatar and have started to build your story, it is time to start creating your unique content.

Your Story

SECTION FOUR

YOUR UNIQUE CONTENT

---

*"You need to create ridiculously good content—
content that is useful, enjoyable and inspired."*

—Ann Handley

What Is Content?

According to the Dictionary Britannica, content (a least for our purposes) is defined as "the ideas, facts, or images that are in a book, article, speech, movie, etc."[6]

It is estimated that there are over 3 billion (yes...with a 'B'!) pieces of new content posted across all the social media platforms every single day. That does not even include new daily content from books, emails, podcasts, videos, direct mail, and other formats.

We, as a global society, are on the internet every day. The internet *IS* content. That is all it is. Just a bunch of information that

---

6   *https://www.britannica.com/dictionary/content*

has been placed on a computer server somewhere in the world for your viewing pleasure.

In the computer world there is a saying: "Garbage In, Garbage Out" or GIGO for short. When you stop and think about all that content out there, the burning question is "Is it true?" If it is on the internet, it must be true... right? Absolutely not! It all depends on who put it out there and if they actually know what they are talking about.

I mean seriously, I have watched enough crime shows on TV in my life that I could pretend to be a forensic scientist, publish a report that sounds completely real with all the little details built in; yet it would be completely fabricated. Made up in my little old head with literally nothing to back it up. And yet someone will read it, believe it, share it and before you know it, I am listed as an expert in forensic science: GIGO.

Or you could use Artificial Intelligence (AI) to create content. AI will spit out a bunch of words based on your prompt, and while it may sound impressive, it will never be uniquely you. At the end of this section, we will get into a bit more detail about AI content. For now, let's just say that if it did not come directly from your brain, based on knowledge you have acquired and that you have confirmed to be true, then it is not true and certainly not unique.

The bottom line is, there is a lot of crap content out there. But if you are a person of integrity (which I believe you are) then you would never create crap content, at least not on purpose. The reality is, the second you place a piece of non-factual content in front of someone and they call you out on it, not only have you lost that person as a prospect, but you have also lost everyone that reads their comments. And that content is out there forever. (Yes, even if you delete it, it is still out there on a server somewhere.)

The goal of content is to attract your target audience to you, your products, and your services. Period. You create it to build trust, create engagement, and differentiate yourself from your competition. As a business owner, if you are not creating new content continuously to drive new people to your products and services, you will never be successful.

Psychologically speaking, humans are drawn to content to which they can relate. Those specific words that speak directly to them. Humans also, for the most part, inherently want to help others. When you share your unique content that incorporates bits and pieces of you (your story), you connect with your audience on a much deeper level. They *FEEL* like they know you.

Great content is all about *FEELING*.

So, what is "unique" content then? Unique content is yours and yours alone. It is crafted in your voice to speak directly to your ideal client avatar. It utilizes aspects of your story and unique experience. It does not come from some template or from an AI app.

When you create unique content, you may include aspects of things already known, for instance, this book includes a lot of information. Some of it you have surely heard or read in some form elsewhere. However, not in this way. This book is my unique way of teaching this information that includes my personal and professional perspectives and all my past experience.

How do you interpret your knowledge and relay it back to your audience? No one in the world has lived life exactly the way you have. No one has the same exact experiences. No one has the same exact training. And even if someone took the same training as you, your interpretation of the material is different based on personal beliefs. When you create authentic content based on your experience, that is your unique content. Your unique methodology. Your proprietary system. Written in your unique style.

There are many different types of content. Let's take a minute to review the main content types.

Content Vehicles

Building a profitable, scalable business requires that you get your message in front of your audience. You do this in the form of content. When you think about it, everything is content, even the words we speak.

Back in the day, direct sell campaigns were delivered by snail mail (sending via the post office), a strategy that is still in use today. But let me ask you, what do you do with all the "junk mail" the post office delivers every day? I don't know about you, but most of mine ends up in the circular file (trashcan, or actually the recycling bin these days).

In the 1980's, email became the main form of communication in businesses and by the 1990's, when computers were becoming popular appliances for the home, everyone started using email to communicate. Back then, the internet was quickly gaining traction. Before we knew it, we were socializing on the internet. In 1997, SixDegrees.com came out as the first social media platform. It was soon followed by others. In 2003, LinkedIn launched as the first business social networking platform. MySpace, also launched in 2003, was the first global personal social media platform. In 2004, Facebook launched, and as they say, the rest was history.[7] Since the early 2000's, there have been many social media platforms that have come and gone and/or evolved into what they are today.

Before the internet, reports and guides were created and printed to be delivered by hand or snail mail. Today, we have blogs, articles, consumer awareness guides, eBooks and other forms of online content that get delivered in seconds. As a global society, we are now dependent on the internet and the millions of programs,

---

7   https://en.wikipedia.org/wiki/Timeline_of_social_media

platforms, and applications to connect with one another and to conduct business.

Speaker venues are all about content. Whether in person or virtual, speeches are nothing but spoken content. This includes the millions of podcasts that are currently available on virtually every subject.

Today, video is the most popular type of content. According to Forbes.com, "In 2024, a notable 90% of marketers using short-form videos plan to either boost or sustain their investment in this content type. This decision aligns with current trends where half of all marketers prioritize video content, particularly the short-form variety, to capture their audience's attention effectively."[8]

Two Main Forms of Content

When it comes to written content there are two main forms to consider: short-form and long-form. To be clear, your content marketing strategy will incorporate both forms, but it is important to know the difference and when it is best to use each.

While both of the forms seem pretty easy to figure out, you would be amazed by the number of people who use the wrong form at the wrong time or on the wrong platform then wonder why their content is getting crickets.

Short-form content is short and to the point. The general rule is that short-form content is under 1000 words. It's best for social media posts, blogs, news articles, emails, reels, videos under 60 seconds, infographics and such.

---

8   *https://www.forbes.com/advisor/business/software/content-mar-keting-statistics/#:~:text=In%202024%2C%20a%20notable%20 90,capture%20their%20audience's%20attention%20effectively.*

The goal of short-form content is to get your message across quickly. It is great for those who like to scroll quickly through a lot of content. They can get a quick tip or some info and move right along.

Some pros about short-form content: it's easy for your audience to consume, it's easy to read on a mobile device, it's easily shared, and its less resource intensive. Short-form content helps you build your social media presence, create engagement and build that all important know, like, and trust with your audience.

Long-form content is well…longer. Over 1000 words and geared toward individuals who are looking to learn something deeper. It is not meant to be skimmed and scrolled by. Longer blog posts, guides, tutorials, webinars, white papers and videos over 60 seconds fall into this category.

Some pros for long-form content include better keyword rankings; it's great for repurposing into short-form content; and it helps establish you as a thought leader in your industry as you have more space to demonstrate your core genius. Long-form content is great for building brand awareness and nurturing leads.

The type of content, short or long, may depend on the platform you are sharing it on. Some platforms have a character limit for posts, like X (formerly known as Twitter) which has a max of 280 characters at present, so short-form content is the only option.

Believe it or not, Facebook allows 63,206 (totally random or what?) characters in a post. That's about 10,000 words. So technically, you could post a small book in a Facebook post. But don't do that. You have probably seen some of the "long" posts on Facebook. Now, they are usually not over 1000 words, however, most people on social media are there to get a quick glimpse at what is going on in their online world. Unless you have written something really compelling in a long post, chances are few people will read the whole thing.

So, when thinking about your content, ask yourself, how well is it working in this abyss we call the internet? Are you attracting your ideal client avatar to your products and services? Is your audience engaging with your content? Are they reacting, commenting, sharing, watching or downloading it?

If not, it is time to learn how to create unique engaging content that will set you apart from the crowd.

It's Not About You

The first thing you need to know about your content is that it has nothing to do with you.

Seriously. Reality check here. The hard truth is that no one cares about you, or me for that matter. They don't care about what schools you graduated from, what certifications you have or even what you want to sell them. All they care about is one thing…

CAN YOU PROVIDE THE RESULT I AM LOOKING FOR?

You may have heard the acronym for the "universal radio station" WIIFM: What's In It For Me? Psychologically speaking, people are basically self-centered. When they connect with you for the first time, whether they state it out loud or think it subconsciously, they are asking themselves, "What's in it for me?"

You may be creating a lot of content loaded with great information, but if it is not the information your audience is looking for, you will never get the engagement you are looking for. Look back on some of your existing content. Is there a lot of "I" language in it? "I did this…I did that…" They don't care. It's time to shift your language from "Me" to "You".

Don't get me wrong, there are appropriate times to talk about yourself, but only in context of what you can do for them. For example, telling your story in order to relate to your audience and create connection and build a relationship.

If you are wondering how to know what they are looking for, the answer is simple…ASK. Ask them on social media or via email. Ask them what result they are looking for with regard to whatever it is you do. Such as, you could create a Facebook post that reads something like this: "If I could provide you one result as a business consultant, what would that result be?" And let them tell you what they want. Once you have what they want in their words, you have the makings for some great, unique content.

A Few Content Basics

Before we get into the nuts and bolts of creating amazing unique content, let's talk about a few content basics.

Always use the K.I.S.S. method when creating any content. (K.I.S.S.: Keep It Super Simple.) According to the Literacy Project[9], 45 million Americans cannot read over a 5th grade level. The average reading grade level is 7th-8th grade. What does this mean? Use simple words and language to keep readers engaged. Most people stop reading once they find complex words.

It is also important to organize your content in a clear and easy-to-follow structure with headings, subheadings, bold text, and bullet points to make it scannable. This helps readers quickly grasp the main points.

There are four styles of writing: expository, descriptive, narrative and persuasive, of which you will likely use a mix. The key is to make it effortless and enjoyable for your audience to read your content.

---

9   https://literacyproj.org/

Expository writing explains a topic or idea. It contains factual information provided in linier, logical format. There is a clear objective. It does not include your personal opinion. New articles are often written in this style.

Descriptive writing is used to help your reader create a visual in their mind of what you are describing. What does it look like, taste like, feel like, sound like? The goal is to provide enough information to pique their interest. Product and services landing pages are often written in this style.

Narrative writing is just what it sounds like, telling a story. There is a main character, a setting and some plot. The format has a structured beginning, middle and end. You can use this format when telling your story. This type of writing is great for case studies.

Persuasive writing is used to influence your reader; but *NOT* to convince them to buy your product or service. Good persuasive writing uses language that evokes emotions. Asking questions is one way to use this type of writing. It will help prompt your reader to think about the topic. You see this format a lot in ads and sales funnels.

Now let's get into creating that content!

The 4 Key Components of Engaging Content

Creating unique, engaging content is an art. Initially, it takes time to learn, but as with learning to walk, once you learn it well you will be unstoppable.

It is important to understand right from the starting gate that content is all about research and testing. Content that works today may not work tomorrow for the same exact audience. Platforms change, economies shift, interests change, and perceived challenges change.

There are four main things that your content must do.

1. Grab their attention

2. Spark their interest

3. Deliver value

4. Give an action invitation

Each of these has one or more key components that, when used correctly, will help you create unique content that sets you apart from the crowd. Let's go through each one of these in detail.

Grab their attention.

I don't know about you, but from the time I get up in the morning, until the time I go to bed at night, I am pretty busy. We are all busy every day. Fun fact: our brains have over 50,000 thoughts coming in and out every day. Most of these are unconscious thoughts and a lot are repetitive thoughts, however, they are keeping your brain pretty active 24/7.

Readers are inundated with massive amounts of content every day. Why would they stop and read what you have to say? If you do not grab their attention right away, they are gone. Your content must interrupt your readers' thoughts and *stop the scroll.*

The first key component of your content, designed to stop the scroll is your headline. Whatever you write in that first line, whether it is the first line of a post, the subject of an email, the title of a blog or article, the name of your webinar, etc., is what determines whether or not the viewer is going to stop scrolling and look at what you have created.

One of my favorite tools is CoSchedule's Headline Analyzer (check out the Resource List in the back of this book for more info.) This tool helps you evaluate your headline to make sure it is written in a way that will create engagement. It is very simple to use. All you do is write your headline, place it in the analyzer and it will give you a score from 0 to 100. The goal is to have a headline that scores over 70, preferably 80+.

According to CoSchedule[10], the best headlines have six common elements.

First, the headline must evoke some kind of feeling. Remember, humans are emotional creatures. We are interested in things that strike us emotionally. We buy based on emotion. Your headline must create some kind of emotional response from the reader if you want them to stop scrolling.

The second element is action. Great headlines have an action verb in them. The verb relates to the subject of the headline or what the reader will be able to do after reading the content. For example: "*Transform* Your Wellness Routine with These 5 Expert Tips and Tricks."

The third is the tone of your headline. There are two schools of marketing. One school pokes at people's pain points to get them to buy. This is done by including negative words like harm, angry, troubling, etc. The other offers a solution without poking using positive words like benefit, brilliant, inspired, etc. While keeping your headline positive is usually recommended, it actually depends on your audience and the purpose of your content. What is the goal of your content? Use the tone your ICA is are more likely to respond to.

The fourth element is the benefits to the reader. Your headline should be clear on how this content is going to help them or improve their life. Give them a reason to want to read more. Using the example from the second element, if your audience is look-ing for ways to increase their health and they read a heading that

---

10   *https://coschedule.com/blog/best-headlines#elements*

begins, "Transform Your Wellness Routine…" you now have their attention.

The fifth element is more of a headline trick; having a number in the headline. Our eyes are drawn to numbers in a sentence. "The five tricks for living a long and happy life" vs "The 5 tricks for living a long and happy life." Chances are your eyes were drawn to the number versus the written-out version. BTW, both of those headlines score the same number on the Headline Analyzer.

The last element is the length of your headline. Studies show that the best headlines average between 11-14 words. If your headline is too short, you may not have enough information to stop the scroll. If it is too long, you can confuse the reader and that will also cause them to scroll on. Remember, your headline is designed to stop the scroll.

Another important component for grabbing attention is using images. Think about how you decide what you are going to read or not read. If you have ever scrolled through Facebook, Instagram, LinkedIn or other social media platforms where there are images, chances are if you see an image that catches your eye, that is what stops your scroll. A blog or article with a great image will interrupt your brain and cause you to stop and check out the information that goes with the image.

But be careful with images. Make sure your image represents your content. Some marketers know that images stop the scroll. They place images on posts and advertisements that have nothing to do with the content just to get you to stop and look. Their goal is to get you to stop with the image then reel you in with the first line of the content. Frankly, when I see a post or ad that does this, I remove it from my feed. If it was posted by a group or individual, they are removed and blocked. Integrity and authenticity are important to me. If a content writer violates either of those, as far as I am concerned, they are gone.

Here are a few examples of catchy headlines with image suggestions:

- **"How to Engage Clients and Grow Your Coaching Business With Your Story."**

  IMAGE IDEA: *A coach standing in front of a small group of attentive clients, sharing their story with passion and enthusiasm. The background could be a cozy, professional setting like an office or a conference room.*

- **"Are You Ready To Make 2024 Your Most Amazing Year In Business Yet?"**

  IMAGE IDEA: *A person standing triumphantly on a mountain peak, looking towards a bright sunrise labeled "2024" in the sky. This symbolizes reaching new heights and setting ambitious goals.*

- **"5 Simple Networking Power Tips to Help You Look Like a Pro"**

  IMAGE IDEA: *Professionals at a networking event, shaking hands, exchanging business cards, and engaging in conversations.*

- **"Learn the 5 Most Powerful Content Secrets for Attracting Ideal Clients"**

  IMAGE IDEA: *A laptop with a content calendar opened on the screen, surrounded by notes and creative tools like pens and sticky notes.*

- **"5 Tips for Building Healthy Habits and Achieving Lasting Weight Loss"**

  IMAGE IDEA: *A person preparing a healthy meal in the kitchen, with fresh vegetables and fruits, and workout equipment in the background.*

Spark Their Interest

According to Samba Recovery[11], in 2024, the average human attention span is 8.25 seconds. They note that this is less than a goldfish's attention span of 9 seconds! Some studies show that the average attention span on Facebook is 2 seconds.

We are in what I call *The Age of Scrolling.*

In order for you to make the desired impact you want for your unique target audience; you first have to get your audience to pay attention to what you have to say. Your headline is designed to do that. But now that you have their attention, you need to keep it. Sparking their interest is all about keeping that curiosity that initially drew them in. Depending on the type of content, there are a few ways to do this.

The first way is by creating an engaging introduction. Those first few sentences set the tone for the rest of the content. The goal is to build anticipation to keep them interested.

Of course, this means something different to everyone. The content itself is the information that your unique target audience is looking for. It is specifically written for them. Remember, it is all about them. Your content must speak to their specific needs, wants and interests to keep them engaged.

For example, if you are a health coach and your target audience is looking for ways to have consistent energy throughout the day, this headline will grab their attention, and the second line will keep them engaged.

HEADLINE: **"Learn how to keep yourself energized all day with these 5 simple steps."**

---

11   *https://www.sambarecovery.com/rehab-blog/*
      average-human-attention-span-statistics

THE SPARK: *"Imagine waking up every day feeling energized and ready to tackle your goals. No more dragging yourself out of bed, no more mid-afternoon slumps. This isn't just a dream—it's achievable, and I'm here to show you how."*

Making a bold claim that surprises or intrigues your audience is another way to keep their attention.

For example, if you are a content marketing specialist who teaches clients how to create a marketing strategy for success, this may catch and keep their attention:

HEADLINE: **"The most important marketing strategy that you will ever learn for massive success."**

THE SPARK: *"If you're not using this strategy, you're leaving money on the table every single day."*

Using FOMO (Fear Of Missing Out) is another way to draw your audience in and keep their attention. In this type of content, you may be talking about some big new trend or even some limited time offer. The intention is to create a sense of urgency.

For example, if you are a personal trainer promoting a new program starting in July and you get this in front of someone who has been struggling with their weight, chances are they will stop and check it out.

HEADLINE: **"Get Exclusive Access to the Ultimate Training Program—Hurry, Spots are Limited!"**

SPARK: *"Don't miss out on this chance to finally get the body you have been dreaming of! We only have 10 spots available for our July 'Change Your Body Change Your Life' program. Sign up today!"*

If you are writing a piece of short-form content, say in a social media post, the attention and spark may be combined. Questions always spark interest. Psychologically speaking, when presented with a question, our brain automatically wants to answer it.

Let's say you are a relationship coach, something like this could be very effective:

"Have you ever had your heart broken?"

If you have ever had your heart broken, I am guessing just reading that line sparked some emotion in you. Couple that line with an image that represents a broken heart, and you will get engagement on your post.

Another strategy is to tell stories that grab your readers' curiosity. Case studies are great for this. Introduce a client who experienced a problem that your audience can relate to. (Don't forget to ask your client for permission before sharing!)

For example, if you are a business consultant who specializes in helping brick-and-mortar businesses grow, something like this may be very effective:

HEADLINE: **"Meet Sarah, a small business owner who turned her struggling bakery into a local sensation using these simple marketing tricks."**

SPARK: *"When Sarah noticed her sales declining, she knew she had to act fast. Here's how she did it..."*

The goal of sparking interest is to keep your audience engaged and make sure they understand where you are going with your content.

From there it is all about value, value, value.

Deliver Value

We live in an age of micro content. It is that short-form, easy to digest, quick hit, get-in-get-out type of content. People want to be able to get what they need and move on.

Short-form content is all about creating engagement, whereas long-form content is all about providing value and building the relationship.

While you can still deliver value in short-form, long-form content is designed for massive value. Emails, blogs, articles, guides, eBooks, etc. are all forms of long-form content whose goal is to share something of value to the reader.

When you deliver value, your audience keeps coming back for more. This is how you build the know-like-trust factor with your audience. It is how you become a credible resource, or as they say today, a "thought leader". Let's face it, the main purpose of your content is to build credibility in order to gain more followers and attract new clients.

Delivering unique value is what sets you apart from your competitors. It inspires your audience. It drives action.

There is a saying in the value-based marketing world that goes "Always give away your best stuff." People often ask me, "Why in the world would I give away my best stuff? Then there won't be any reason for them to purchase my program!" Here's the thing...the most important person reading your content is that person who fits your ideal client avatar description and does not know who you are yet.

It's easy to write content for people who already know, like and trust you. Heck, for them, you can even toss out a piece of crappy content and they will still engage because they know you. The thing is, it is the ones who do not yet know you that you are looking to connect with. They don't know you from a hole in the wall and they certainly have no reason to trust you. So how do you move them from complete stranger to raving fan? By giving them something of value for free that solves a problem they are currently experiencing. Or gives them some valuable insights for something they want or need.

Trust me, no matter how much you give away, you have more to share and if they are your target audience, they *WILL* want more.

Let's expand on one of the examples from the last section. This could be in a blog or article that is posted to social media, or a guide placed on a landing page so you can capture the name and email address of the reader.

HEADLINE: **"Learn how to keep yourself energized all day with these 5 simple steps."**

THE SPARK: *"Imagine waking up every day feeling energized and ready to tackle your goals. No more dragging yourself out of bed, no more mid-afternoon slumps. This isn't just a dream—it's achievable, and I'm here to show you how."*

THE VALUE:

1) GET QUALITY SLEEP:

WHY IT MATTERS: *Sleep is the foundation of your daily energy levels. Quality sleep allows your body and mind to recover. You wake up refreshed and ready to go.*

ACTIONABLE TIP: *Establish a bedtime routine that promotes relaxation. This could include reading, taking a warm bath, or practicing meditation. Turn off all electronics at least one hour before bedtime. Aim for 7-8 hours of sleep each night.*

2) DON'T JUST FEED YOUR BODY, FUEL YOUR BODY:

WHY IT MATTERS: *The food you eat is your body's fuel. Eat a balanced diet rich in whole foods that will give you sustained energy throughout the day.*

ACTIONABLE TIP: *Start your day with a nutritious breakfast that includes protein, healthy fats, and complex carbohydrates. Examples include a smoothie with spinach, banana, and almond butter or a bowl of oatmeal topped with berries and nuts. Avoid processed and high-sugar foods that lead to energy crashes.*

3) ALWAYS STAY HYDRATED:

WHY IT MATTERS: *Dehydration can cause fatigue and lower your cognitive function. Keeping hydrated helps maintain your energy levels and overall well-being.*

ACTIONABLE TIP: *Carry a water bottle with you and make a goal to drink at least 8 glasses of water a day. Add a slice of lemon or cucumber for flavor if plain water is too bland. Drink water consistently throughout the day, not just when you're thirsty.*

4) EXERCISE REGULARLY:

WHY IT MATTERS: *Exercise boosts your energy by increasing blood flow and oxygen to your muscles and brain. It releases those feel-good chemicals in your brain and helps regulate your sleep patterns.*

ACTIONABLE TIP: *Find an activity you enjoy, whether it's walking, yoga, or a dance class, and aim for at least 30 minutes of moderate exercise most days of the week. Even short bursts of activity, like a 10-minute walk during your lunch break, can help maintain a high level of energy.*

5) PRACTICE MINDFULNESS AND STRESS MANAGEMENT:

WHY IT MATTERS: *Chronic stress drains your energy and affects your overall health. Mindfulness practices can help you stay centered and reduce stress.*

ACTIONABLE TIP: *Create a morning routine where you include some mindfulness techniques such as deep breathing exercises, meditation, or journaling. Taking a few minutes each day to focus on your breath or just reflect on your thoughts can make a big difference to your energy and mental clarity.*

By adding some of these simple shifts in your daily routine, you'll find yourself more energized, focused, and ready to face the world head-on every day. Your journey to sustained energy starts now—take the first step today!

Okay, that was a long example, but it is a great one to model. If you are a health consultant, helping your clients create more sustained energy throughout the day, you not only just gave your reader some information, but actionable steps they can implement immediately.

When someone from your target audience who has never heard of you reads this, they are very likely going to start following you for more tips and tricks. When they implement some of the suggestions and start seeing results, they are going to want to know how they can get more results just like this. And, of course, you have a signature program that expands on all of those tips and more!

This leads us to the last thing your content needs: *The Action Invitation*.

The Action Invitation

This is your Call To Action (CTA). Outside of getting your ideal client avatar to stop and read what you have to say, this is the most important part of your content.

Believe it or not, it's not always obvious to people to take the next step. They read your content, but if there is no CTA, they move on. We all have so much going on in our head 24/7 that we literally don't think about taking action unless someone tells us to. The action invitation is just that—an invitation to take some form of action. The type of action depends on the purpose of your content.

Here are a few examples of CTA's:

- **Comment "Me" below.** This is great for social media posts.

- **Click here to join our private Facebook group.** This one can be used pretty much anywhere.

- **Click here to visit our website.** Blogs, articles, and email are all good places to share your website.

- **Click here to download your free guide.** This can be used in social media, website, video content and more.

- **Click here for a free 30-minute strategy session.** This one is best combined with long-form content.

One mistake a lot of coaches and consultants make when writing a CTA is asking their prospect to "Click here for a free 30-minute strategy session!" too soon. If I don't know, like or trust you yet, that is like meeting someone for the first time and asking them to marry you on the spot. Not gonna happen! I mean, everyone knows that a "free strategy session" is code for "sales call", right? Now, as the people writing this CTA, we know that is not true, but *they* don't know that, yet.

Do you know what a sales funnel is? If you have ever clicked on a site that said they had something of interest for a very low cost, and you clicked on it, only to find that once you say, "Sure, I'll try this for $7!" Then before you can check out, you get the "*BUT WAIT!*" and they offer you something else…and something else. Before you know it, $1000 is charged to your card and you wonder how that happened.

My dislike of sales funnels story is for another time. The reason I bring it up is because that same model can be used for something more productive, your CTA.

Let me explain the *CTA funnel* using our previous example.

You create a new guide and write a social media post something like this:

> *The Image*: A person who looks happy and full of energy enjoying a beautiful day. (Grabs their attention.)

Post Content: Imagine waking up every day feeling energized and ready to tackle your goals. No more dragging yourself out of bed, no more mid-afternoon slumps. This isn't just a dream—it's achievable, and I'm here to show you how.

I just created a guide called "Learn How to Keep Yourself Energized All Day with These 5 Simple Steps."

If you would like to be one of the first ones to get your hands on this informative guide, comment 'Guide' below and we will send it directly to you!"

Asking them to type "Guide" in the comments is the first CTA in the funnel. It's simple and non-intrusive. They either enter the word in the comments, or they don't. If they do, you send them the link to a landing page where they enter in their name and email address to get instant access to your free guide. (See what we just did there? Now they are on your email list. You can continue to build the relationship!)

They download your guide, read the amazing information and now, after reading what you have written, they know a little more about you, who you are and what you do. They now know, like and even trust you because you have just given them something of value that is exactly what they were looking for. They want to know more. They may not be quite ready to marry you yet, but they are definitely interested in what you have to say.

At the end of your guide, there is another CTA. This one is moving them further down the CTA funnel.

The Guide CTA: "If you have been struggling with yo-yo energy levels and are ready to stop the madness, click here for a free quiz that will help you identify why your energy is what it is and will give you suggestions tailored specifically for you and your unique situation."

The quiz may live on your website or its own specific landing page. Once again, you have not tried to sell anything yet. All you are doing is providing more value and letting them get to know you.

Once they complete the quiz, they enter their email in again to get their results AND now you have a new CTA that might be something like this:

> *"Hey <name>! Your complete results are on their way to your email box. Here is a quick summary. <List the info here>. Based on your results, we may have a few more suggestions that could help you keep your energy levels steady all day. If interested, click here to schedule a free 15-minute quiz result review with one of our energy specialists. I promise you this is NOT a sales call! There is no obligation and no gimmicks. We just want to help you find the energy you need to live a happy and productive life."*

When they call, stay true to your word and don't make a sales pitch. Listen to their story and learn a bit more about them. This helps you decide if they are actually a good fit for your program. At the end of the call, ask them if there are any additional tools or resources they need that would help. If they say no, that simply means they are not quite ready yet to commit to anything. Keep them in your group and on your email list and keep providing value. If they say they are looking for something, you can now let them know that you have something that may be of interest to them. Ask them if they would like to hear about it. Again…. this is not selling, rather it is offering a solution to their problem.

Not forcing a sale on a prospect is another way you set yourself apart from the crowd.

So, now that we have all of the pieces put together for writing unique content: 1) Grab their attention, 2) Spark their interest, 3) Deliver value, and 4) Give them an Action Invitation; let's take a look at some specific platforms and start putting this into practice.

Content Platforms

Social Media Content

In the world today, the majority of people have an account on at least one social media platform. According to Backlink[12], as of February 2024, there are over 4.95 billion people using social media worldwide.

As of April 2024, there are 15 different social media platforms to choose from, but for our purposes we are going to focus on the main 3 that most businesses use to connect with their audience: Facebook, Instagram and LinkedIn. Note, these strategies work across all platforms.

Current stats show that Facebook has over 3 billion active users and is ranked as the #1 platform; Instagram has over 2 billion users and LinkedIn has 875 million members and over 1.6 billion visitors on the platform each month. Chances are pretty good that your target audience is on one of those platforms!

When it comes to the type of content you post, the platform matters. Your unique business will determine which platform is best for your content. In the end, chances are you will be sharing content on a few different ones.

In this section, we are specifically talking about text content. We will get into video content a bit later, where we will also talk about the #2 ranked platform—YouTube—that has over 2.7 billion active users.

The first thing to know is that each platform has its own text posting requirements and restrictions.

---

12   *https://backlinko.com/social-media-users*

As mentioned previously, a Facebook post can be up to 63,206 characters long which is roughly 10,000 words. Instagrams limit is 2200 characters, which will give you roughly 400 or so words. LinkedIn has a limit of 3000 characters. These limits include spaces and punctuation, so how you write your content matters.

Truthfully speaking, you never want to hit the max limit on any platform. The limits are set for the specific type of audience and generally speaking, if you have reached the max, your post is way too long. You will likely not get the engagement you are looking for, no matter how good the content is.

Remember, there is short-form and long-form content. When posting on social media, short-form content is the best. Remember, short-form is described as content under 1000 words. That is generally less than a standard blog post.

Consider those posts you have seen on Facebook that seem to go on forever. They look long in post format, but chances are they are well under the 1000-word short-form length. Just for giggles, I went out and copied a bunch of those longer Facebook posts to check the word count. They came in between 120-250 words. The point is social media platforms are for short-form content. Long posts rarely get read through completely on social media unless they have extremely compelling information.

The goal of your content is to attract your ideal client avatar and turn them into a raving fan. On these social media platforms, that means they are engaging with your content by clicking one of the reactions, commenting and sharing. If your post is long, it must capture the readers interest, or they will be gone in a flash.

While we are talking about engagement, let's stop and chat for a sec about those pesky algorithms. The goal of every social media platform is to create a great user experience, which means users are engaging with the content they view.

Every social media platform has their own unique algorithm. An algorithm is basically a program that has a set of rules and signals that rank your content. The algorithms also analyze users' behavior, their interests and interactions to understand what the user likes. This is why when you check out something on social media and engage (click a reaction, comment, etc.), it seems that magically you start seeing more similar content. The algorithm says "Hey, they like this type of information. Let's find some more to show them."

With your content, the thing is, if you create posts and no one engages, the algorithm will show less of your content, and you will not even know about it unless you check your analytics. We'll talk more about analytics in the next section. For now, the thing to understand is that your social media content is all about engagement. If your content is not getting engagement, you need to change things up.

The last comment I will make on algorithms is that they change constantly. Don't even bother trying to keep up with them. Just know there is something in the background watching your content and deciding whether or not to show it to more people. Seriously, I don't think anyone, even the platforms themselves, understand what they are doing! Just keep an eye on what is working and do more of that. If it stops working, change your content to see what is now working.

Let's get back to the content.

There are **five main social media content categories** for posts that you can mix and match to keep your audience coming back for more.

The *first* is the PERSONALITY POST. Showing your personality in your content humanizes your brand and helps create a stronger connection with your audience. Here are some things you can post to get your followers to feel like they're getting to know the real you.

- Behind-the-scenes glimpses of your life and business
- Your favorite books, music, movies, and hobbies
- Share personal anecdotes, achievements, and challenges
- Fun facts to showcase the unique aspects of your personality

The next time you are out on social media, check out which posts are getting the most engagement. Chances are pretty good they are personality posts. These are the posts that share something personal, like family, pets, kids, vacation shots etc. They connect with the audience because they see you are human, just like them. They evoke emotion. This helps your audience begin to know, like, and trust you on a deeper level.

Second, we have the VULNERABILITY POSTS. When you open up about your vulnerabilities, you create a safe space for others to do the same. This helps you create deeper connections within your community. This is also the key to creating raving fans. People connect with feelings, emotions, and stories that they can relate to.

Here are some ideas for this type of content.

- Share your thoughts and feelings on relevant topics or current events in your industry.
- Tell stories that describe who you were before you became who you are now.
- Explain a struggle you experienced and describe how you overcame it.
- Open up about your fears, or insecurities, and share how you're working through them. We all have them.
- Acknowledge a difficulty your audience may be facing and offer words of encouragement and support. Ask questions to make them reflect on their own feelings and experiences. For

example, you could ask a simple question like "Have you ever had one of those days when you seriously wonder why you went into business in the first place?"

Third are the CONTRIBUTION POSTS. There are two types of posts in this category. The first is about your **organization's contributions and philanthropic activities,** how you give back to your community. Your followers want to know that you're a good person and good people tend to pay it forward. There are many ways your organization may give back, including:

- Setting aside a portion of each sales proceeds to a favorite charity
- Volunteering at a local non-profit
- Creating a scholarship for one of your programs

Posts that showcase how you give back help to show your audience that you care. (Remember, it's all about the emotion!)

The second type of post in this category is to **highlight members in your community**. Their contributions to the group. When you celebrate and highlight community members you show your commitment to building a supportive community. People want to know that you really care and that you take the time to uplift others.

These types of post might include:

- Spotlighting members who are engaging most in your private Facebook group page.
- Celebrating members who have accomplished something, like publishing a new book.
- Your members philanthropic activities.
- You can create a monthly Member Spotlight where you highlight a community member and let the group know what they do.

The *fourth* post category is the CREDIBILITY POSTS. These posts reinforce your reputation and credibility as a trustworthy source of information and expertise. If you want to grow your business, you need to become an authority in your field. Let's face it, you can talk about what you can do and provide tons of value, and yet it is that one time *someone else* says how good you are at what you do, that everyone starts paying attention.

Here are a few things you can share to increase your credibility:

- Client testimonials
- Case studies
- Specific industry credentials
- Share industry and personal awards

Another thing that increases your reputation from 0 to 100 is partnerships. If you do a business event or interview with a high-level person in your field, people will immediately trust you more. Let's say you provide investment advice. Would your content engagement and sales increase if you did an interview with Warren Buffet? Absolutely! Okay...that may be stretching it a bit. But you can find people in your industry who are one or two levels up from where you are and interview them.

The *fifth* and most important category for social media post are the VALUE POSTS. Delivering value should be at the core of your content strategy. Value Posts are a great way to showcase your expertise. By providing continuous value, you show your audience that they matter and that you are here to help them find the solutions they are looking for.

At this point you should know your ideal client profile well enough that you can deliver content specific to your audience's needs and desires.

There are infinite ways to provide value, but here are 5 that will increase the likelihood of people moving from lead to client and become loyal supporters of your brand.

- Offer practical tips and actionable advice.

- Provide links to how-to guides, informative articles, or videos that teach your audience about a relevant topic or concept in your industry.

- Share solutions to common challenges.

- Share resources like apps, tools, spreadsheets, or websites that can help your audience achieve their goals or make their life much easier.

- Ask for feedback or suggestions. Create surveys to see exactly what they are looking for. Then, create content based on the results of your research and deliver as much value as you can to solve their needs.

Using all five of these categories is one way to keep your audience engaged and coming back for more. It is part of a content marketing strategy that will set you apart from your competitors.

Let's talk about IMAGES. First, Facebook and LinkedIn do not require that you have an image with your content. Sometimes, a post without an image can get a lot of attention as long as you have grabbed their attention with an awesome headline. Instagram, however, is an image-driven platform which is why the character count is lower than the others, so an image is required. On Instagram, the image trumps the headline at the attention grabber.

When it comes to images, you want to make sure the image you include does two main things:

1. It grabs attention.

2. It is related to the content.

There is this thing out in the internet world called "click bait". Have you ever stopped at an ad while scrolling Facebook because the image caught your attention and then you clicked on the image only to find that it had absolutely nothing to do with the content? That, my friend is a form of "click bait". They are baiting you with the image. Don't do that.

Images that spark emotion always stop the scroll. Pair that with a catchy headline and you will have the readers' full attention.

In the back of this book there is a *Useful Resources* section with apps and resources that will help you with all your content marketing creation. For images, I personally love Canva. Their free app will handle pretty much all of your content design needs. And their paid app, which is very cost-effective, has a ton of tools, templates, designs, photos and more to help with just about every aspect of content marketing.

It's time for you to put some of this into practice. In the next section, *Section Five—Your Unique Content*, we will be putting this all together. For now, here is an exercise to get your creative juices flowing for your social media posts.

> EXERCISE: Use the space here in the book or take out a sheet of paper and define 5 topics for each of the 5 categories listed above. Voilà! You now have the start of 25 posts. That should cover your social media posting needs for an entire month!

PERSONALITY POSTS:

1. _____

2. _____

3. _____

4. _____

5. _____

VULNERABILITY POSTS:

1. _____

2. _____

3. _____

4. _____

5. _____

CONTRIBUTION POSTS (PICK A COUPLE OF TOPICS FOR EACH TYPE):

1. _____

2. _____

3. _____

4. _____

5. _____

CREDIBILITY POSTS:

1. _____

2. _____

3. _____

4. _____

5. _____

VALUE POSTS:

1. _____

2. _____

3. _____

4. _____

5. _____

> PRO TIP: If you are lacking ideas to use as topics, this is a great time to tap into AI for ideas. ChatGPT, Gemini, Claude or any of the text-based AI apps are your research friends!

Helpful guides, blogs, articles, and other resources.

There are two approaches in marketing: the traditional "push" marketing, where companies push their products and services on you (ick!) and the "pull" approach where a company builds the know, like, and trust with the audience so customers come to them organically.

The next type of content we want to dive into includes all of the different types of value-based content designed to "pull" your audience closer to you. It is that content that you create and deliver for free that allows you to showcase your expertise. It is often the first step in building the know-like-trust factor with your prospective client.

This type of content is generally referred to as a "lead magnet". It attracts your exact target audience and provides them with tangible information that helps them in one way or another. It allows your prospect to check you out and *leads* them closer to you. It allows them to see if you have the solution they are looking for and whether or not they resonate with your unique mentoring style.

There are some very valuable benefits of using lead magnets, including:

- ATTRACTING THE RIGHT AUDIENCE: By offering a lead magnet that is relevant to your target audience, you can attract the right people to your business who are genuinely interested in what you have to offer.

- BUILDING YOUR EMAIL LIST: Every lead magnet includes the four key content components formula, including number four: the Call To Action (CTA). Depending on the type of lead magnet, your CTA may be for the reader to subscribe or "opt-in" to a newsletter by sharing their name and email address, or you might create a guide that is delivered via a landing page where the prospect enters their name and email address on a form in exchange for the document.

- ESTABLISHING CREDIBILITY AND AUTHORITY: By offering a valuable resource, you can establish your credibility and authority in your niche or industry. These also help to build trust with potential customers which will make them more likely to do business with you in the future.

- INCREASING CONVERSIONS: Once your prospect has your lead magnet, you can then nurture the relationship with the potential customer through email marketing and ultimately convert them into paying customers.

Lead magnets can be long or short-form content; though, the longer the content, the better the opportunity to connect with the prospect and provide a result that has them wanting more.

Lead magnets should include the following elements which include the four key components:

- A CLEAR AND COMPELLING HEADLINE: Your lead magnet should have a clear and compelling headline that grabs the reader's attention and communicates the value of the content.

- VALUABLE CONTENT: It should provide valuable content that addresses a specific problem or need that your target audience has. It should offer a solution or answer a question clearly and concisely. Remember, your content is all about what your ICA wants, not what you want to teach. Refrain from using "I" language. Create content that is speaking directly to your ideal client using "you" and "your" personal pronouns.

- ATTRACTIVE DESIGN: The design of your lead magnet should be visually appealing and professional-looking. It should be easy to read and include images, graphs, or other visual elements that enhance the content. If the lead magnet is meant to be printed, be mindful of the format and make sure it can be printed without using up all their printer ink.

- BENEFITS-FOCUSED LANGUAGE: Create content that focuses on the benefits the customer will get by taking action on the information inside the lead magnet.

- CALL-TO-ACTION (CTA): Your lead magnet should include a clear and prominent CTA that encourages the reader to take the next step, such as subscribing to a newsletter, signing up for a webinar or scheduling a consultation.

- CONTACT INFORMATION: Include your contact information—website, email address and if appropriate, your phone number—in your lead magnet so that potential customers can easily get in touch with you should they have any questions or want to learn more about your services.

There are literally hundreds of lead magnet formats. We are going to cover a few of the most common types here. The type that you will create will be based on your unique business and what makes the most sense for your target audience.

Let's begin with the shorter form lead magnet. It could be a tip sheet, a simple checklist, template, worksheet, or any other piece of content that is generally no more than a page or two.

Tip sheets and checklists are short, focused resources that outline key steps or tips for achieving a specific goal or outcome. They are simple, fast, and effective ways to attract your target audience and get them to engage with you. For example, if you are a life coach, you might create a habit tracker that helps your audience track their current habits to see where improvements can be made. Because they are easy to create and share, you will likely have multiple tip sheets or checklists that you circulate to your audience regularly.

Here are the steps for creating a tip sheet or checklist type of lead magnet.

STEP 1— RESEARCH YOUR TOPIC.

A tip sheet or checklist helps your unique target audience solve a problem or specific need. *Research your topic.* This is not about you showing the world what you know. It is about providing a result your audience needs. Check your ego at the door and ask your audience what they need. If you use social media, you can create a post in your community asking what their current biggest challenge is. Based on the responses, pick one of the common problems they identified, and create a tip sheet or checklist resolving that problem.

For example, if you are a fitness coach and your audience tells you their biggest problem is staying motivated and on track with their fitness plan, you can create a daily checklist to help keep them motivated and engaged with their routine.

STEP 2 — CREATE THE CONTENT.

Develop the content for your tip sheet or checklist, including the key steps or items that your audience needs to know. Make the content concise and easy to understand.

STEP 3 — DESIGN THE LEAD MAGNET.

Create a visually appealing design for your lead magnet that is consistent with your brand. Use colors, fonts, and graphics that resonate with your audience and make the lead magnet easy to scan. Microsoft Word and Canva are both good tools for creating visual design.

Make sure you have included all four of the main content components. A catchy headline, something to spark interest, some valuable information that will help resolve a problem and a CTA. Note, for these short lead magnets, your CTA could be something simple like visiting your website for more information.

Next, we have **templates and worksheets**. You can offer a free downloadable template or worksheet that helps your target audience achieve a specific task or outcome. For example, a bookkeeper may want to create and share a budgeting template that helps their audience keep track of their business expenses.

The steps for creating a template or worksheet are similar to the tip sheet and checklist steps.

STEP 1 — RESEARCH YOUR TOPIC.

A template or worksheet provides a fillable document on a topic that your target audience needs to work out or organize. The question is what do they need? Remember, the purpose of a lead magnet is to provide your target audience with something of value. Consistently doing so will help your prospect feel comfortable with you and build the know-like-trust factor. Pay attention to what your target audience is asking for.

> TIP: Your target audience is out on social media every day asking for help and guidance. Pay attention to what they are posting. It is easy to find a topic that you can convert into a template or worksheet.

For example, if you are a marketing specialist and your audience is interested in organizing their social media content, you could create a social media content calendar template that will help them create clarity around their marketing content.

STEP 2 — DEVELOP THE CONTENT.

Develop the content for your template or worksheet. Include the key elements or sections that your audience needs to fill out. Make the document easy to understand and actionable.

Provide clear instructions on how to use the template or worksheet. This will help them get the most value from your lead magnet.

STEP 3 — DESIGN THE LEAD MAGNET.

Create a visually appealing design for your lead magnet consistent with your brand. Use colors, fonts, and graphics that resonate with your audience and make the lead magnet easy to use.

You may want to create a protected, fillable Microsoft Word document or use Google Docs or a spreadsheet tool like Microsoft Excel or Google Sheets to make it easy for your prospect to fill in the blanks. If you have access to Adobe Pro (paid version) you can create a fillable PDF.

For the four types noted above and other short-form content lead magnets, there are two more steps that are common to both.

STEP 4 — OPTIMIZE FOR LEAD GENERATION.

The purpose of these "freebies" is to turn your cold leads into warm leads and begin to build the relationship. Since these types of documents are usually shared via social media, email, etc. rather than from a landing page with an opt-in form, your CTA should encourage your audience to sign up for your email list, subscribe to a newsletter, join your Facebook Group, or do some other action that will keep them engaged and allow you to nurture the relationship.

STEP 5 — PROMOTE THE LEAD MAGNET.

Share your lead magnet via email, on your website, social media, and other marketing channels to attract attention and generate leads.

Utilize other people's audiences (OPAs). On Facebook there are many groups that allow you to share. Most only allow sharing on certain posts. Connect with groups where you know your ideal audience hangs out and share your content whenever possible with their audiences. You never know where your next big client is hanging out!

These types of lead magnets also make great giveaways for podcasts, webinars and websites. The goal is to get your them in front of as many people as possible.

The steps are pretty much the same for all of the smaller types of lead magnets. Again, there a many different types of short-form documents you can create. It all depends on what your audience actually needs. A few other types of short-form content include resource lists, tool kits, planners, facts sheets, etc.

Let's move on to the meatier content: the **guides, articles, blogs**, etc. This is the long-form content where you have lots of room to really show your prospects exactly what you do, how you do it in your unique style. The goal is to create a piece of content so informative that, if this is the one thing they ever get from you, it is enough to help them decide immediately whether or not you are the perfect fit for them. And, by the way, this helps you make sure the potential new client is a good fit for you as well. After all, you are looking for your ideal client avatar, not just anyone with a credit card…right? (Please tell me you said "Right!") Those who download, read and act on the CTA are likely perfect clients for you.

Just as with the short-form lead magnets, there are many different forms of long-form ones. We will cover a few of the most common, including guides, eBooks, blogs and articles.

Guides and eBooks are the most common type of lead magnet to attract new clients. Because of the length, you can pack a lot into them. In Joe Vitale's book, *Hypnotic Writing*, he notes "As a general rule, the more you tell, the more you sell." Guides and eBooks allow you to showcase your knowledge without "giving away the farm" as they say. Good long-form content gives the reader some practical, tangible information that can be put immediately into practice. And it also leaves the reader wanting to know more. I personally believe every coach or consultant should have at least one informative guide to share with their audience. Think of it this way, your signature lead magnet is the content that leads them to your signature program.

Here are the steps for creating a **guide or eBook**.

STEP 1 — DETERMINE YOUR TOPIC.

I cannot reiterate this enough…it is not about what you want to tell people, it is about what they want to know. Your content is all about them. A great guide or eBook topic is something that the majority of your audience is looking for. If you are a health coach, it could be something like "10 Steps to Transform Your Health and Wellness" or for a business consultant, "Uncover Top 10 Myths About Entrepreneurship". You want to pick a topic that is interesting and has longevity. The short-form docs are easier to create. These long-form ones take a bit of time, and you don't need a lot of them, so the more relevant your topic, the better. If you are not sure if you have the right topic, try it out on your audience. Go on Facebook or LinkedIn, create a survey with your top 5 topics and let the audience tell you which one they want most.

STEP 2 — CONDUCT YOUR RESEARCH.

Once you have determined the topic, it is time to conduct research. This research can include reading articles, conducting interviews, reviewing case studies, and gathering statistics. The more research you conduct, the more informed your guide or eBook will be. Make a list of research topics that correspond with your topic. Ex. Do you need statistics added to your content? Do you need quotes from other relevant resources? Using outside resources to back up your own content gives the document more credibility.

STEP 3 — CREATE AN OUTLINE.

Using your ideas and research data, create an outline. It should include main topics, subtopics, and any supporting information or data. The outline is meant to help you organize the information and make sure it flows naturally.

STEP 4 — WRITE THE CONTENT.

Now that you have your outline, it is time to start writing content. Use your research and outline as a guide and ensure that your content is well-organized and easy to read. Use a tone that is appropriate for your audience and avoid using overly technical language. Remember what we said about the reading level being 7th-8th grade at best, so keep the words simple.

Make sure you have incorporated the four key components:

1. A captivating headline to grab their attention.
   - "10 Steps to Transform Your Health and Wellness"

2. The sub-headline can be used to spark interest.
   - "Unlock Your Best Self with Practical Tips for Lasting Change"

3. Provide massive value!

4. Your Action Invitation (CTA).

STEP 5 — ADD VISUALS.

Adding visuals to your guide or eBook can help break up the text and make it more visually appealing. Find a front page visual that works with your headline to grab your readers' attention. Inside the guide, visuals may include images, charts, graphs, and tables.

STEP 6 — PROOFREAD AND EDIT.

After you have written your content and added visuals, it is important to proofread and edit your work. Check for spelling and grammatical errors, ensure that your content flows well, and make any necessary changes. If you have a friend or colleague that can proofread for you, that is even better. They may catch something that your eyes miss. They can also give you feedback on the content.

STEP 7 — DESIGN AND FORMAT.

Once your content is finalized, it is time to put it all together. Choose a design that is visually appealing and reflects your brand. Ensure that your content is easy to read and navigate.

There are many apps you can use to format the content. Some of the more popular include Microsoft Word (you can create from scratch or use a Word template) and Canva, which allows you to create a document that can be downloaded in PDF format for distribution. Check the *Useful Resources* section in the back of this book for more options.

STEP 8 — PUBLISH, PROMOTE & FOLLOW-UP.

Guides and eBooks, work best on a landing page for promotion. A landing page is a one-page website where your lead will go, enter in their name and email address (and possibly phone number) in order to get access to your document.

There are a few specific characteristics of a good landing page including:

- A long-tail domain name
- A great heading
- Single-focused topic

- One-page design
- A 30-second or less instructional video
- The download form

A long-tail domain name

A long-tail domain name is different than a regular website domain name. It contains multiple words or phrases, usually more than three, and is very specific to a particular niche or topic.

For example, www.fromoverwhelmedtooverjoyed.com

The above example includes words that this particular target audience is searching for. Long-tail domains can also help your page appear higher in web searches.

A great heading

The first thing a visitor sees when reaching your page is the landing page heading. Your heading is the one line that will either hold the viewer's attention and get them engaged or cause them to leave your page without taking action.

> NOTE: For your guide landing page, the headline and sub headline should be the title and sub-title of your guide.

EXAMPLE: *How to Avoid the 5 Biggest Mistakes New Coaches and Consultants Make.*

The headline above was created and refined using the Headline Analyzer free version. A great headline incorporates a combination of uncommon words, emotional words, and power words to attract your ideal audience.

Just as important is the sub-headline; this is the line that comes after your headline that motivates your visitor to take action and download your document.

> EXAMPLE: *Learn How to Move From Overwhelmed to Overjoyed in Your Business.*

This sub-headline combined with the main headline engages your target audience to give you their contact information.

Single-focused topic and one-page design

One landing page, one topic. The purpose of a landing page is to capture your visitor's attention and get them to share their contact information in exchange for your lead magnet.

Do not add social media links or anything else to this page. Keep your visitor solely focused on the topic. You do not even need your logo on the page. The sole focus is your guide. Inside your guide, you have contact info and your logo.

On a computer, the user should not need to scroll down to see the information. The content on the landing page should be on a single screen.

A 30-second or less instructional video

Create a 30-second video telling the visitor what it is and how to get it.

For example, a short script may be as follows:

> *Hey there, are you a coach or consultant who's feeling a little overwhelmed or frustrated with your business right now? If so, enter your name and your email over on the right and download a free guide that will show you how to avoid the five biggest mistakes that most coaches and consultants make in their business. Move yourself from overwhelmed to overjoyed in your business again.*

The download form

The most important part of the page is the form. This is where your visitor will enter their name and email address, which will be saved in your CRM, in exchange for the document.

Most forms now include the phone number. This is useful if you want to do text reminders. Most visitors will not be comfortable giving you their phone number if they do not already have the know-like-trust factor with you. For this reason, you may want to have only the Name and Email as required fields on the form and the Phone as an optional field.

Once the form has been completed, the user should have immediate access to your assets (eBook, guide, video, etc.). They should not be redirected to another page to access it. K.I.S.S.

> NOTE: Always include a spam policy on your form.

EXAMPLE: *"We hate spam as much as you do, and we promise not to sell or rent your information."*

Publish your page and promote it

Once the page is completed, it is time to publish it and share it with the world! Share your lead magnet page on social media and email. Anywhere you can share the link to your landing page. Utilize other people's audiences. Don't be shy. If you are a guest on a podcast, your lead magnet makes a great freebie to give away, and having the landing page makes it easy for you to share and build your email list.

> NOTE: If you are not landing page savvy and cannot create your landing page, you can hire a freelancer on FIVRR or UpWorks, or any of the other freelance sites to do it for you very cost-effectively.

Blogs and articles are another way to display your expertise and establish authority in your industry. This type of content can even help increase your chances of being invited to speak at events. There are speaker event planners who are always on the lookout for engaging speakers. Creating this type of content can help you get recognized as a thought leader in your industry to get you invited to speak in front of your exact ideal audience.

If you have a website, a blog is a must. The internet search engines (Google, Edge, etc.) have complex algorithms that rank websites. This is why you see certain websites on the first page of your search instead of being buried three pages down. The ones that rank higher are the more active sites. Adding a blog to your site each week helps to keep your site active and hence, higher ranked.

If you use LinkedIn, articles are a great way to establish credibility. Just like a blog, you want to consistently post a new article each week. They are great for extended visibility across the platform.

Magazine editors are often looking for new articles to publish. Look for magazine publications that are in your industry and see if they accept new articles. Research industry publications that speak directly to your target audience.

When it comes to blogs and articles, use a more narrative or descriptive type of writing. The same rules apply for this content:

- Know your audience. Make sure the topic is something that helps solve a problem or gives them some tangible advice.
- Create a catchy headline.
- Provide massive value by giving tips or insights that the reader can implement immediately.
- Include a Call-To-Action
- Include appropriate images. Blogs should have a cover image that relates to the content. Magazine articles usually allow two to three related images depending on the publication.

Let's talk about SEO for a moment…

What is SEO? It stands for Search Engine Optimization. In the simplest, layman terms, SEO refers to the specific words people are searching for online. The "keywords" that are used in the search bar. It could be one specific word or a phrase. When writing content, especially blogs and articles, you want as many people to find you as possible. Using keywords throughout your content signals the search engine that your content is related to what users are searching for.

Using links in your blog or article is another way to rank higher. If you are referencing another person's work or a tool, etc., adding a link to their site can help your content get found easier.

With blogs and articles, it is all about consistency. If you decide to publish a blog on your website, make sure you create a schedule to upload a new blog once a week. If you write an article on LinkedIn, you'll also want to consider a weekly publication. For magazines, it depends on the publisher's schedule. Most magazines are monthly publications.

Similar to the short-form lead magnets, the steps are pretty much the same for all of the long-form ones. Again, there a many different types of documents you can create. It all depends on what your audience actually needs. A few other types of longer form content include white papers, case studies, email courses, etc.

In the next section, Section Five—*Your Unicorn Factor*, we will talk about creating a specific content schedule just for you and your unique needs.

Okay! It's your turn.

1. Pick one of the shorter types of lead magnets—a tip sheet, checklist, template or worksheet. Whichever makes the most sense for your audience and come up with 3 topics that provide

your audience with something of value that they will want to download immediately.

Topic 1:

_____

Topic 2:

_____

Topic 3:

_____

2. Identify three topics for your long-form signature lead magnet. While it depends on your audience, topics that include lists almost always work best. For example, *"The 5 Most Important Weight Loss Secrets that You Need to Know."*

Topic 1:

_____

Topic 2:

_____

Topic 3:

_____

REMEMBER: *it is okay to ask your audience. Come up with the three topics and then share them with your audience. Ask them which one would be the most useful for them.*

Email Content

Now that you have that rocking lead magnet helping you build your email list, let's talk about email content. Using the email list you have begun to build with your guide or some other lead magnet, you now must nurture the relationship. It's all about gaining that know, like and trust with your potential new client.

According to Porch Group Media[13], in 2022 there were over 4.258 billion active email users worldwide. It was predicted that the number of email users will grow to 4.4 billion by 2024. They also note there are over 7.9 billion email accounts worldwide. So, email marketing still has its place in the business world and it should definitely be part of your unique marketing strategy.

First things first…if you want to be recognized as a "real" entrepreneur, you need a "real" email address. Gmail, AOL, Yahoo, Me… are not professional email addresses. Your business email address should be yourname@yourdomainname.com. If you want to be taken seriously as an entrepreneur, make sure you look professional. To accomplish this, you first need a company domain, like www.autumnascent.com (that's me!). Once you have that, you can set up a domain email address. Most domain registration sites offer email services as well. Companies like GoDaddy and NameCheap offer email options so you can set up an email address that goes with your domain like regina@autumnascent.com. It is not necessary to have a website created to set up your domain email address, you just need a business domain name.

The next thing you need for your email management is a CRM, Customer Relationship Management application. We could write an entirely new book on how to set all of this up and what programs are best, but here is the highlight version. There are a lot

---

13   https://porchgroupmedia.com/blog/100-compelling-email-statistics-to-inform-your-strategy-in-2023/

of CRM applications out there. Some do everything: they manage email, let you create landing pages, have membership sites and more, all included in one package. Applications like Kartra, Kajabi, and Highlevel are examples of all-in-one solutions. But these can get a bit pricy. If you are just starting out, there are more cost-effective email management systems like MailChimp and MailerLite that allow you to set up email campaigns and manage your contacts. Check out the resources in the back for more info on CRM solutions. For now, just understand that when you capture emails from your contacts, you have to have some place to manage them.

Okay...back to the email content.

Before we get into the regular, everyday type of email content, let's go back to that lead magnet you created. The one that has the landing page. Once someone enters their information into the form, you deliver your lead magnet, you now want to start building a relationship with your prospect. The form where they entered their contact information is connected to your CRM. Inside your CRM, you set up an *automation sequence*, also known as a "drip campaign" where you "drip" additional information to keep the audience engaged. It is essentially a series of pre-written emails sent automatically on a schedule. The drip campaign starts the minute they hit enter on the form and send you their contact information.

Here's a simple drip campaign example:

- DAY 1: Immediately after they enter their information in and hit enter: Send a welcome email. Deliver the lead magnet and thank them for downloading.

- 3 DAYS LATER: Send a value email. Share a helpful tip or resource related to your lead magnet.

- 5 DAYS LATER: Share a personal story. Tell a personal story that relates to the guide content. Show them your human side.

- 7 DAYS LATER: Send the final automation email that sums up the lead magnet content.

When creating the emails for the automation, use the subscriber's name and any other information you have to make your emails feel more personal. This helps build a stronger connection. Pay attention to feedback from your subscribers. If they're not engaging with your emails or downloading your lead magnet, find out why and make improvements.

Also remember that each one of these emails follows the general content rules. Generally speaking, just like with other types of content, people will skim through an email instead of reading every word. The subject line is your "headline". It should grab their attention. The first couple of lines in the email should spark interest. Then you provide some additional value related to the download. Lastly, you include a CTA. The more interesting the email, the more likely they will read the entire thing.

The first drip email in any lead magnet automation is just making sure they received their guide. Nothing else. No additional info or CTA. Simply stating "Hey %First Name%! We all know that 'tech happens' so I just wanted to make sure you got your download. If not, click here to download it now." That's it. Nothing fancy in this one.

The other three emails should all have a CTA that is strategically placed in your P.S. Remember the CTA funnel? This is a perfect place to put it into full action. In the Value email, the CTA should be something simple like having them join your private Facebook group or join you on LinkedIn etc. At this point, they are just getting to know you. They are a cold lead. Your goal is to build the relationship, so you want to move slowly. Don't ask them to marry you on the first date!

In the Personal Story email, your CTA may be another lead magnet. Possibly one of the smaller ones that has something to do with content in the guide. For example, if your guide is "10 Steps to Transform Your Health and Wellness", you may give them a Habit

Tracker Worksheet to help keep track of their daily habits or maybe a Bedtime Checklist for a Great Night's Sleep.

The CTA funnel in the drip campaign builds as you establish know, like and trust. By the time they get to the last email, they should be pretty familiar with you and what you do. If they have read your guide and the subsequent emails, you have their full attention. They have graduated into a warm lead. So, the last CTA could be a free 30-minute consultation where you can answer any questions they have about their unique situation.

This is the end of the lead magnet email drip campaign, but it is not the end of the relationship! You have their contact information. In order to stay top-of-mind, you want to continue to nurture relationships with all of your email contacts. This is accomplished by creating an email marketing strategy that makes sense for your unique business. It may be sending out one email a week or more. It could be a newsletter, a value-based email, or something else that will keep the audience engaged.

Just be aware of how many emails you are sending. If you send too many, it is like *The Boy Who Cried Wolf* syndrome, they keep seeing your name on the emails and they get so many that they just stop paying attention to them. In your CRM, keep track of the number of people who unsubscribe from your email list. If a large number of people are unsubscribing, you are either sending out too many emails or your email content is not interesting enough for them to stay engaged.

Just as with drip emails, all subsequent emails you send should include the four key components. Always make sure your subject line (headline) grabs attention. I don't know about you, but I generally have over 100 new emails coming into my email accounts on a daily basis. Most of them are junk or spam. I decide which are important by answering these two questions: Who sent it? and Is the subject line something of interest to me? A catchy subject line will always make me stop and open the email to see if it is something I want to read in full. The first couple of lines of the email is what will spark my interest. If I am not interested, it gets deleted.

Personalize all your emails. Your CRM (no matter which one you use) has a way to automatically add the first name of the email contact. Different CRMs may use different formats for this, but it will be something like "Hi %FIRSTNAME%,". This will take the first name from the contact information and add it to the email, so it looks more personable: "Hi, Regina,".

Remember the content key component flow. If you send emails and start right in telling the recipient what you are offering (CTA), chances are they are going to close and delete the email quickly. And possibly unsubscribe. Make sure that the first couple of lines pull them in and sparks interest. Again, if you have a lot of emails in your mailbox, you are likely scrolling through and not really reading them all, just like you do on social media. You are waiting to see something (a catchy subject line) that makes you stop scrolling and engages you.

One etiquette comment here on subject lines. *DO NOT* put Re: or FW: on a new email. Some marketers use this to trick you into thinking that someone is responding to something you sent to get you to open their email. Faking your audience into reading something is not a good way to build a relationship. Similarly, refrain from using fantastic phrases like "You won't believe what I just found out!" or "My team is going to kill me for giving this to you!" as subject lines. Again…ick!!

Write your emails so they are skimmable. You have my attention. Now get to the point. One email, one focus. Make it easy to read and don't put a bunch of images or emojis all over the place. A single image, if appropriate, and a couple emojis (if any) for effect are enough. Some email providers will flag emails with images as spam, so use them sparingly.

Always, always, always include a P.S. This is where you repeat or insert your CTA. Many savvy email readers skip right down to the P.S. immediately because they know that is where you get to the real point of the email. Every email should have a CTA that is appropriate based on the content of the correspondence. If your email is about The Top 5 Tips for Attracting New Clients to Your Business (subject), your P.S. CTA may be something like "P.S. Are you ready to attract more clients? Click here to book your free 30-minute consultation now and get personalized advice tailored to your business needs!" The "click here" should be a link to your booking calendar.

With so many users now reading their emails on their phones, make sure your email is optimized for mobile viewing. This means, if you don't need to use an image, don't. It just takes up unnecessary space. Unless your image is something like a flyer for an event, no image is best.

Under your P.S., you may also want to have a consistent footer that links to your social media locations and website. You can use the icon pictures for each location (e.g., Facebook logo) that links to your pages. This is a constant reminder for them to connect with you.

At the very bottom of all of your emails you must have an unsubscribe or "opt-out" option. This is required to comply with the CAN-SPAM Act in the United States on all commercial emails. Other countries have opt-out laws as well. It allows the recipient to opt-out of future emails. Your CRM should have this automatically at the bottom of your emails. Commercial emails also must have your business address on them to comply with anti-spam laws. This can be a P.O. Box or a physical address. Again, depending on the CRM you use, once you've set up your profile information, the opt-out may be automatically included by the CRM in all emails you send.

A note of warning…If you do not comply with the anti-spam rules, your email may be blacklisted. This means that you will no longer be able to send or receive any emails from that email address. The only way to get off of a blacklist is by trying to contact the support team for the blacklist that blocked you. This is usually ineffective and the only real way to get off the list is to wait until some time passes and they automatically release it, which could be a long time. If you are not sure if your email has been blacklisted, you can use this tool—MXToolbox—to check the status of your email address. It will let you know if you have been blacklisted and tell you exactly who did it. The moral is, avoid being spammy with your emails. Make sure the recipient can reply to your email. Do not use "no-reply" email addresses. Do not manually add people to your email list. You must have their written permission. Always have them opt-in to your list by providing their contact information on a form.

This brings us to our final (for here at least) content medium, your video content.

Video Content

Video content is another form of lead magnet that includes Instagram reels, Facebook stories, Facebook Lives, YouTube videos, webinars and more.

If you want to become known for what you do in today's world, you must create videos. It should be an integral part of your content marketing strategy. According to many research studies, the human brain can process visuals faster than text. With video, your audience gets to know the real you faster and deeper than any text based medium. According to Adobe[14], "In 2024, video content is one of the best ways to create impactful marketing campaigns that

---

14   https://www.adobe.com/express/learn/blog/video-marketing

increase customer engagement and retention." And that's exactly what we are looking for.

As mentioned, YouTube is ranked as the #2 most popular platform with over 2.7 billion active users. Let's face it, when you break something and need to fix it, where do you go? YouTube! Semrush[15] noted that in 2023, YouTube was the second-most visited website in the world. It doesn't matter who your target audience is, trust me, they have searched YouTube at one time or another for help or information.

Before we get into creating video content, let's talk about equipment. Sure, you can go out and purchase really expensive video cameras, microphones, lights, greenscreens and more, *OR* you can simply use your cell phone or computer to create your videos. Does it make a difference? With today's technology, it really doesn't. You do need to make sure you have decent lighting. This can be accomplished using natural light from windows or strategically placing lamps. Ring lights are not very expensive and if you purchase a clip-on ring light, you can position it just about anywhere. (Just Google "clip on ring light")

If you have a laptop, there's a built-in camera that will usually do the trick, or you can purchase a webcam like a Logitech C920 for under $70. Instead of using your computer's microphone, purchasing an external one is a good idea, especially if you have a lot of background noise. You don't need to get super fancy here. You simply need a basic USB clip-on microphone that can be purchased for under $20. Why clip-on and not Bluetooth? Because there are many things that can interfere with wireless devices. Having a hard-wired device guarantees your sound is consistent. Oh, and a word about ear buds…they don't look professional. And they can do a lot of damage to your hearing. All you need to do is get set up and test your environment by creating a few videos. Then play them back to see what needs to be adjusted.

---

15   *https://www.semrush.com/blog/youtube-stats/*

If you are a bit antsy about going live on video, here's my simple advice…. *JUST DO IT*. The more you do, the more comfortable you will be. If I saved all of my out-takes (the videos I did not publish because they were really that bad) I would need a new storage drive for my computer! When I first started out, I was scared to death of the camera. A friend gave me the very same advice I now give you: just do it. I did. I messed up. I did it again. I messed up again. Then I got better and better. Now, I love going live and creating videos. You will too, trust me!

Okay, let's start with the short-form content videos. These are the reels, stories and even short Facebook Lives. One burning question many people have: What's the difference between a reel and a Facebook story? According to Facebook[16] "Stories on Facebook can be used to share everyday moments with friends, followers and people you've chatted with on Messenger. Stories are only visible for 24 hours, but you can always revisit stories you've shared in your story archive." "Reels on Facebook are short-form videos that can include music, audio, AR effects, and other options. You can watch reels from creators and make your own reels to share with friends around the world."

Stories and reels can be used to post videos of personal or business-related information. We won't get into the specifics about creating stories and reels here. There is more than enough information between Facebook's Help Center and Meta to give you the step by step you needed to create your videos. We will, however, cover what to put in your short videos for the most impact.

Let's focus on reels since they can be viewed by a much larger audience than personal story posts. It's basically the same structure for stories.

---

16   *https://www.facebook.com/*
      help/1026380301307372/?helpref=uf_share

When it comes to video content, the same rules apply as with text content. You want to follow the four key content components. At present, reels can only be up to a maximum of 90 seconds long. So being clear and concise with your message is very important.

Now, you can share all kinds of information on a reel. For our purposes here, it's all about sharing valuable content to help you stand out as an expert in your field:

1. To grab the viewers' attention, add a headline or caption to your reel. Doing this actually ranks you better with the algorithms too.

2. To spark attention, the first few seconds of your video are the most important. There is a "3 second rule" with Instagram reels. If a viewer does not watch for 3 seconds or more, it doesn't count as a view. Jump right into the meat of your content. Don't beat around the bush. Remember, you only have a maximum of 90 seconds to get your message across.

3. Provide 20-30 seconds of real value. Something your audience wants to know.

4. Give them a call to action by asking them to comment, like or share.

Some additional tips for reels.

*   Do your research and include keywords in your script.
*   Longer is not always better. Consider the attention span of your audience. You can actually pack a lot of information into a 90 second reel. Shorter (under 30 seconds) may be better for more views.
*   Use hashtags to get more views. There are some great hashtag generators that can help you identify tags that are highly searched. You can even drop your script into an AI app like ChatGPT and ask it to suggest hashtags for you.

- Reels that talk about contests and giveaways are great for engagement.

- Take your reel and share it to your Facebook story for more reach.

- You can take a reel and embed it in a blog or on your website.

At this point you may have noticed a theme, eh? When it comes to creating content, no matter the type, you're including the four key components. This goes for Facebook Lives too. A Facebook Live is just what the name implies. You go Live on your Facebook business page or group page and provide some value to your audience.

If your audience is hanging out on Facebook (which they tend to do) Lives are a great way to build rapport with them. They want to know the real you. Lives are super easy to create and all you need to do is show up and just be you. These are not fancy, highly scripted videos. Just pick a topic and chat Live in your Facebook group or business page.

Your content, like all content, must be something that audience wants. Make sure it is engaging. The best way to go Live on Facebook is to create an event. This way, you can invite specific members of your community to watch and comment during the broadcast. If you do not create an event and simply "go live", members of your audience will receive a notification in their feed (as long as they have not turned notifications off!) They may or may not see the notification while you are Live. If you create it as an event, you are giving them a heads up that you'll be Live so they can plan for it.

When it comes to Facebook Lives and your unique content marketing strategy, it's good to go live at least once a week for 5-10 minutes. You may decide to go live with a weekly theme. For example, if you are a Life Coach, you may pick a theme such as gratitude, or mindfulness and talk about what they mean and give some tips. A Live is basically a mini-training. The key is consistency.

The algorithms love video content that gets engagement. Here are a few things to consider for a Facebook Live:

- Create your Live as an event and give it a title that will attract your audience. If you're a business consultant and you decide to have a weekly "Tips & Tricks Tuesday," create the heading that includes a topic to attract your viewers. Such as *Tips & Tricks Tuesday—How to Attract More Clients Using Email Marketing.*

- Introduce yourself and the program name (Tips & Tricks Tuesday) at the beginning of each Live.

- Create an outline of what you want to cover so there is a flow to the content. Don't just wing it.

- Don't worry about mistakes or stutters. The purpose of these Lives is for your audience to get something of value and get to know you. So, be you. Don't try to be perfect. No one is.

- Ask the audience to comment during your Live to spark engagement.

- Ask the audience to put #Live if they are watching you Live and #Replay if they are catching the replay.

- Don't go Live too often. Once a week is generally good. If you go Live too often, people will lose interest.

- Ask your viewers to engage by typing in the comments. This not only keeps your audience engaged, but it also keeps the algorithm engaged.

- At the end, include some call to action that is appropriate based on the content.

- Finally, thank them for watching and say goodbye.

For example, I do a Live Tips & Tricks Tuesday every week. I open with "It's time for Tips & Tricks Tuesday. I'm Regina Andler and this week we're taking about … <insert topic here>". At the end of the broadcast, I usually say "That's what we have for this week. See you next time on Tips & Tricks Tuesday. Bye for now!"

Of course, the content for your Facebook Lives depends on your unique business and your unique audience. The goal is to give them a little bite of information from your Live, so they get something of value and also get to see and hear the real you.

Now let's chat about the long-form video content. Videos over 10-15 minutes are generally considered long-form. This means you could create a longer Facebook Live, a free mini course or webinar. Long-form videos give you more time to fully explore a topic. They are great for educational content and tutorials.

But remember that attention span we have referred to a number of times? We (us humans) have a lower attention span than a goldfish. What does that mean for long-form content, whether text or video? It had better be something very interesting to your audience otherwise they will be moving on in a flash!

You have a unique business, complete with your unique story and unique way of coaching. A long-form video is the perfect showcase for this. If you are looking to establish yourself as a thought leader in your industry, long-form video is where you can really shine. The key is picking a topic that resonates with the majority of your audience. It needs to be something they really want to know about. Something that will hook them into your world, so they'll begin to follow you, join your community, and your email list.

There are a number of long-form video mediums to consider, including free webinars delivered by a landing page (similar to your guide), live webinars, challenges, and even podcasts fall into this category.

For our purposes here, we will talk about the most common type of long-form video content: the webinar. Webinars come in a of different names including "workshops", "masterclasses" and seminars. I tend to prefer the term "masterclass." "Workshop" sounds like too much work and that doesn't sound very appealing. "Seminar" sounds a bit too formal and also doesn't sound like fun. With the term "masterclass," you are insinuating that the participant is going to come out with some new, important knowledge that can be put to use immediately in their life or business. That sounds much better, at least to me.

Webinars are a great way to showcase your knowledge and build rapport with your audience. There are two ways to deliver this type of content. The first is using a static, "evergreen" (meaning the content has long-term relevance) recorded video that can be shared over and over again. The second is a live webinar. Which is better? It depends on your audience. Both have value and you can even get creative. Do a live webinar, record it, then share it as an evergreen webinar: 2 for the price of one!

According to LiveWebinar[17] "The average attention span of an adult is about 20 minutes, so it's no surprise that the average length of a webinar is also about 20 minutes. If your webinar is too long, you run the risk of losing your audience's attention." A lot of webinars go from 30 minutes to an hour. It has been my personal experience that anything over 30 minutes is too long. These are free, value-based events that you share to build your audience and attract new clients. I suggest keeping your long-form video content to 20–30 minutes for the best results.

So, let's talk about your unique webinar content.

With a live webinar, engagement is key. Whether you are delivering the webinar via a Facebook Live, Zoom, or a webinar platform like WebinarJam, you have the ability to interact with the audience which extends their attention span.

17   https://www.livewebinar.com/faq/other/
     what-is-the-average-attendance-rate-for-a-webinar#

Chances are pretty good you can give a webinar on a variety of subjects within your industry. The first thing to determine is your goal for the webinar. Is it to educate? Demonstrate? Inspire? The most important thing to consider is your audience. Make sure you have a clear objective, then make a list of webinar topics and ask your audience to rank them. Which one is the most popular? That's the content to focus on.

In considering our four key content components, the title of your webinar is the headline and must be designed to attract the exact audience you are looking for. When sharing information about the upcoming event and creating a landing page for participants to register for the live presentation (or to get access to an evergreen webinar), your headline is what grabs their attention and gets the initial engagement going. Make it sensational! For example, if you are a health coach, something like this may work: "*Feel Better, Live Better: Transform Your Health in Just 30 Days*". What you write for the description is what will spark their interest and get them to register.

There is a defined structure to webinar content. First, is the introduction where you introduce yourself, your credentials, the topic and what the audience will get from participating. Then there's the meat of the webinar, the main content where you'll provide that massive value. Break down the main points into sections with clear transitions. Lastly, the conclusion, where you summarize key takeaways, provide some actionable advice and, of course, give them a call to action. You'll be surprised by the amount of content that can be packed into a 30-minute webinar.

Setting up a webinar takes a bit of time. Let's go through the process step-by-step:

1. Determine the primary goal of your webinar (lead generation, education, product demonstration, etc.). Then identify the target audience. Remember, the real goal is to deliver unique,

engaging content that helps convert prospects into clients. Give them what they want, not what you want to share.

2. Choose a webinar platform. If you have never done a live webinar, do some research to determine the best platform for your event. Compare the various webinar platforms like Zoom or webinar specific apps like WebinarJam, or you can even set up a simple Facebook Live. Just pick the one that works best for you and your audience.

3. Pick a topic that addresses your audience's interests and needs. Create an outline and write a script for your presentation. Include all four key components in your content. Note interaction points as well. For example, you can ask your audience to enter a number in the comments or chat if they agree with a point you made. Add these engagement pieces into your script so you'll remember to prompt your audience.

4. Schedule the webinar. Select a date and time that is convenient for you. If you have a local audience, it will be easy to pick a time. With a country-wide or international audience, there will always be people in time zones where it's not a convenient time. So, offering a replay option is a good idea for a wide-spread audience. Plan the duration of the webinar so you can let people know how long it will be when registering for the event. If you are planning to teach for 30 minutes and then have a 30-minute Q&A session, make sure the audience knows that the total duration will be 1 hour.

5. Create a registration page. Set it up with all of the details about the webinar, including the topic, date, time, and benefits of attending. This is a standalone page, not on your main website. Include a form for the participants to fill out with their name and email address that will be fed into your CRM and flags each as a participant of this live webinar.

6. In your CRM, set up an automation to let the participants know where to go for the Live event. Leading up to the event, you can send emails with information about the event to the participants. On the day before and on the day of the event, send emails letting them know it is almost time to start and remind them where to go. I generally send a reminder email 24 hours before the event, 1 hour before and one last email at start time.

7. Promote your webinar like crazy! Send invitations to your email list, post on social media, and ask friends and colleagues to share the details and a link to the registration page. Visit networking groups locally and online. Use those OPAs (Other Peoples Audiences) we mentioned before. Check out podcasts and other places where you can share your information.

8. Prepare your presentation. There are two schools of thought here. You can create slides that enhance your content, or you can just be on screen without slides. I personally prefer slides that illustrate the points being made with my content. This helps those who are visual learners get more out of the event. For more engagement, you can plan to use polls or have a live Q&A session at the end.

9. Rehearse. Live webinars can be scary for some. Rehearsing your script will help you be more confident delivering the content. Just remember, you will make mistakes and that is okay. We all do! Make sure your internet connection, audio, video, and any other equipment is working properly. You can even do a dry run to make sure everything is good to go.

10. Set up and test the webinar platform. If you are going Live on Facebook, and have never done a Facebook Live before, now is the time to go out and play around with a few test Lives to make sure you know what to do. Then set up a Facebook event page for the webinar. If you are using a third-party platform, like Zoom, configure the meeting information. For example,

on Zoom, you may want to "mute all" on entry to the event and possibly set up the meeting with a waiting room so you control when the participants can enter the meeting room.

11. On the day of the live webinar, test your connections and equipment. Log in to the platform 10-15 minutes before the start time to make sure all your tech is working properly. *Don't forget to hit the Record button!* Deliver your presentation confidently, sticking to the planned content and timing. Engage with your audience throughout the entire webinar.

12. After the webinar is over, use your CRM to send a thank you email with the key takeaways from the content to everyone who registered. If you promised any resources, include them in the email. Share a link to the recording in the email for those who want to go back and watch it again and for those who registered but could not make the live presentation. Ask for feedback.

13. Analyze the webinar performance. Check out the registration and attendance data, engagement metrics, and feedback to assess the results.

I know, it sounds like a lot, because it is. Planning and presenting a live webinar is a project. Any long-form video content takes a bit of work to set up and present if you want to make the biggest impact. The effort is totally worth it in the end.

So, what about YouTube; that #2 ranked platform that we talked about? You can't actually create videos on YouTube; however, your brand-new recorded webinar can be uploaded to YouTube. Once it's on this platform, providing you have an attention-grabbing headline (title) and have strategically inserted some popular keywords, you can be found by anyone anywhere in the world. There are over 4.95 billion monthly active users on YouTube. I am sure some of them are looking for exactly what you have to offer.

One really cool tool I like to use for sharing video content (both short and long) is an app called StreamYard. This app allows you to stream across multiple platforms at one time. So, you can go live on Facebook, LinkedIn and YouTube simultaneously. How cool is that. It works with other platforms as well. Check out the *Useful Resources* Section for more information on StreamYard.

Other long-form content follows basically the same process. The key is creating something of interest. When you do, that is when your videos go "viral". Meaning you are getting noticed. People are viewing, reacting and sharing your content, making you and your company very popular.

It's your turn! Answer this one question:

What is a topic that provides something of value to your unique audience you could talk about for 30 minutes without any preparation?

Picking a subject for a Facebook Live, a webinar or other video format (whether short or long-form) that you know by heart will help you easily create content and present it in a confident manner. This will prove to your audience that you know your subject and helps establish you as a thought leader in your industry.

Unique Content and AI

We can't have a conversation about content these days without bringing up the elephant in the room—Artificial Intelligence (AI). Kind of sounds like an oxymoron, yes? How can content be unique if it is created by a machine?

Let's get one thing straight, AI is here to stay. It is ingrained in your daily life right now and you may not even know it. Do you use Siri? Alexa? Do you watch Netflix? Guess what? All of these are AI based applications. AI tools have been ingrained in our society for a while now and they are just going to grow more and more.

No, it is not going to take over the human race! Could it take away your job? There is a saying on the streets today, "AI isn't going to replace you, but someone who knows how to use it will." If you want to have a successful business, you need to know at least something about AI, especially when it comes to marketing content. If you don't you will likely be left in the dust by your competitors who are using AI. So, if you have not done it already, it is time to jump on the AI bandwagon.

Do you ever sit at your desk, staring at your screen thinking, "What the heck am I going to post about today?"

AI is fantastic for helping you come up with ideas and doing research! Sure, you could go out to Google (or whatever browser you use) and ask for information, but all you are going to get is a list of sites that have to do with your request. Now you have to go in and out of the sites looking for what you need. OR, you can go to AI, ask the same question i.e. "Give me 10 topics to use for Facebook posts on healthy eating" and AI will give you exactly what you ask for in seconds.

If you are trying to figure out what to put in your guide or webinar, you can ask AI to create an outline for you. It can even create the guide or your webinar script!

You do not need to have a technical background to learn how to use AI to create *unique* (yes, I said that!) content. You just need to know something about "Prompt Engineering," a really fancy term that simply means how you "talk" to AI. Once you know that, then you can virtually (pun intended) create anything with AI. This is another one of those subjects that could be its own book, so I am just going to cover the basics of Prompt Engineering here to get you started.

There are two main Prompt Engineering styles, conversational and one-shot:

- Conversational is just what it sounds like. You are having a conversation with the AI tool you are using, such as ChatGPT, Claude, Gemini, etc. to get the response you are looking for.

- One-shot means you enter one very specific prompt to get the exact result you want.

Understand one thing, if AI does not give you the results you are looking for, it's not AI's fault, it's yours. AI is still just a machine, a robot. It is giving you a response based on your request. If you did not get the intended result, it means you were not clear on your instructions. The good news is, you can just keep drilling down and adding more clarity until you get what you are looking for.

If you ask AI "Please create a guide that talks about how to live a healthier life," you will likely get some okay information. Not unique, but okay. AI is going to pull the most popular things it finds and spit them out on the page for you. It may be a good start, especially if you are having trouble coming up with content. But the result will not be unique, and certainly not in your voice.

If you want good replies from AI, you need to learn how to ask AI for the information. Here are the 5 main elements of a good AI prompt:

1. IDENTITY: You need to tell AI what their role is. For example, "Act as if you are an expert nutritionist."

2. REQUEST: This is where you tell AI what it is you want them to do. Be specific. "Your job is to create a guide that provides an audience of women over 50 years of age with the 5 most important tips on how to live a healthier life using simple changes to their diet."

3. CONTEXT: Give AI any additional information outside the request. It could be information on the steps you want AI to take to gather the information ("Pull the information from the latest trends."), a summary context ("Add a call to action..."), etc.

4. GUIDELINES: Specific instructions for how you want the output (result) to look like. For example:

   a. Use bullet points under each section

   b. The tone is casual

   c. The reading level is seventh grade

   d. Separate each section of the guide to make it easy to read

   e. Suggest an image for each of the sections

5. EXAMPLES: If you have a reference, give AI an example of what you want the output to look like.

Here's what a prompt might look like:

IDENTITY: *Act as if you are an expert nutritionist.*

REQUEST: *Your job is to create a guide that provides an audience of women over 50 years of age with the 5 most important tips on how to live a healthier life using simple changes to their diet.*

Expand on each of the tips with actionable advice.

CONTEXT: *Include a cover page and an intro page at the front of the guide. Add a call to action at the end that has them book a free consultation call using this link: www.bookyourcallnow. com.*

GUIDELINES:

   a. *Use bullet points under each section*

   b. *The tone is casual*

   c. *The reading level is seventh grade*

   d. *Separate each section of the guide to make it easy to read*

   e. *Suggest an image for each of the sections*

I entered this prompt into ChatGPT and the tool created a complete outline with usable content that could now be cut and pasted into a Canva document to create a new guide in less than an hour.

Sure, there are some pieces that may need to be rewritten. Unless you enter very specific instructions for the introduction, you will want to update that. You may or may not want to change some of the tips. If you have 5 specific tips in mind for your guide, you'll want to tell AI what they are in the prompt, so it knows exactly what you are looking for. The bottom line is, the more specific the request, the better the result. Every AI prompt, no matter what AI tool you are using, should have the first 4 main elements. If you do have an example, like a previous guide you created, the output will be even better.

> PRO TIP: Use a Word document or Google Docs, etc., to create your prompt detail, then cut and paste it into the AI prompt. Save your prompts so you don't have to keep recreating the information.

Try it! Open up one of the AI tools, like ChatGPT, Claude or Gemini (all have free versions) and play with some prompts. The more you play, the better you will get.

Okay, it's now time to polish up that horn! Let's define Your Unicorn Factor.

SECTION FIVE

YOUR UNICORN FACTOR

"Well, now that we have seen each other," said the unicorn, "if you'll believe in me, I'll believe in you."

— Lewis Carroll, *Through The Looking-Glass and What Alice Found There*

Putting It All Together

If you've been playing along, you are clear on your unique business, your unique audience, your unique story and you've set the stage for creating some really great unique content. Your unique qualities will now all come together to help you set yourself apart from the crowd.

Let's face it, the coaching and consulting industries are pretty saturated. The only way to make it in today's world is by standing out. And to do that, you need a plan.

Your Unique Strategy

Sorry, I can't tell you what your unique strategy should look like. I don't know enough about you or your business, yet. You see, your unique strategy is just that, unique to you and your specific situation. For some, all the content they ever have to create will be on social media. For others, it may be all via email. Some may only need content that is presented live, via speaking engagements. Your strategy depends on your unique audience.

Back at the beginning, when you were identifying your unique audience, one of the things you discovered was where they hang out. That knowledge will give you the starting point for figuring out which content mediums and platforms you should be creating content for. You want to be where your ideal audience resides; otherwise, even your best content will flop.

Your audience is likely using multiple content mediums and platforms. The question to ask is where do they primarily hang out? If that's Facebook, start there. If that's LinkedIn, start there. If it's email, start there. You get the picture. Then identify the second most common place. Most people have at least one social media account and an email address. This is how you start defining your unique content strategy.

While I can't create a specific unique strategy for you without knowing more about you and your business, I can give you a starting point. Here's a simple, 6-step framework to get you started:

1. KNOW YOUR AUDIENCE: This is the foundation of your content strategy. You need to understand:

    a. **Who are they**: Their age, job, income level, interests, and values?

    b. **What problems do they have**: What keeps them up at night? What frustrates them daily?

    c. **What solutions are they looking for**: How do they want their life or business to improve?

To get this info, you can:

a. Survey your existing clients or email list

b. Look at comments and messages on your social media

c. Check out online forums where your audience hangs out

d. Have one-on-one conversations with people in your target market

2. CHOOSE YOUR PLATFORMS: Not all platforms are right for every business. To decide which platforms are best for your audience:

a. Look at where your unique ideal client spends their time online

b. Consider which platforms suit your content type (e.g., YouTube for videos, Instagram for visuals)

c. Think about where you're most comfortable creating content

d. Start with 1-2 platforms and master those before adding more

Remember, it's better to be great on one platform than mediocre on five.

3. SET YOUR GOALS: Your content should have a purpose. Common goals include:

a. Getting more clients or customers

b. Building brand awareness

c. Establishing yourself as an expert in your field

d. Growing your email list

e. Increasing engagement with your audience

f. Driving traffic to your website

Pick 1-2 main goals to focus on. This will help you create more targeted content.

4. PLAN YOUR CONTENT: This is where you get specific about what you'll create. Consider:

    a. What topics will you cover? Make a list of themes related to your expertise.

    b. How often will you post? Be realistic about what you can consistently manage.

    c. What types of content will you create? (blog posts, videos, podcasts, etc.)

    d. Can you batch create content to save time?

    e. How will you mix promotional content with value-based content?

A content calendar can be really helpful here. Plan out your content a month in advance.

5. CREATE AND SHARE: This is where the rubber meets the road. Tips for this stage:

    a. Set aside dedicated time each week for content creation

    b. Use tools to help you create and edit (like Canva for graphics or AI tools for writing)

    c. Don't aim for perfection. "Done" is better than perfect

    d. Share your content across all your platforms

    e. Encourage your audience to share your content too

6. MEASURE AND ADJUST: This step is crucial for improving over time. Here's how to do it:

    a. Decide which metrics matter for your goals (likes, shares, click-throughs, etc.)

    b. Use analytics tools to track these metrics

    c. Look at your numbers regularly (monthly is a good start)

d. Notice trends. What topics get the most engagement? What times of day do your posts do best?

e. Do more of what works and less of what doesn't

f. Be willing to try new things and see how they perform

It's normal for some content to flop. That's how you learn and improve.

By following these steps and continuously refining your approach, you'll develop a content strategy that's uniquely suited to your business and audience. It takes time and effort, but the results will be worth it. You'll build stronger connections with your audience and attract more of the right clients.

You may be wondering how much content to create. Too little, and you may not connect with your audience. Too much, and you may desensitize them, so they stop paying attention. The amount of content depends on your audience. Content creation is a constant process of trial and error. Here is a good guideline to start with:

1. SOCIAL MEDIA:

    a. Start with 3-5 posts per week on your main platform. If you completed the exercise in the *Your Unique Content* section, you should have 25 posting topics all set and ready to go

    b. Mix it up with text and images

2. LEAD MAGNETS:

    a. Create 1-2 high-quality lead magnets every quarter

    b. These could be eBooks, checklists, or short video courses

    c. Make sure they solve a specific problem for your audience

3. EMAILS:

    a. Send 1-2 emails per week to your list

    b. Include valuable tips, not just sales pitches

    c. Keep them short and easy to read

4. REELS:

    a. Start with 2-3 reels per week

    b. Keep them short (15-60 seconds) and focus on a single tip or idea

    c. Use trending audio or music to increase visibility

    d. Include text overlays for viewers watching without sound

5. VIDEOS:

    a. Aim for 1-2 videos per month if you're just starting

    b. These can be live streams or pre-recorded content

    c. Keep them under 10 minutes unless you're doing a deep dive

Remember, quality beats quantity every time. It's better to create less content that really helps your audience than to churn out lots of so-so stuff.

One last thing to keep in mind: your content strategy is not set in stone. As you learn more about your audience and what they respond to, you'll want to tweak your approach. That's normal and good! The best strategies evolve over time.

The goal isn't just to create content, it's to create quality content that helps your audience and moves your business forward. Every piece of content should either educate, entertain, or inspire your audience, preferably all three!

Don't be afraid to show your personality in your content. That's part of what makes it unique. Your audience isn't just buying your services; they're buying you. Let them see the real you in your content.

Finally, be consistent. It's better to post regularly on one platform than to try to be everywhere and burn out. Start small, be consistent, and grow from there. Your unique content strategy is a marathon, not a sprint.

Research!

I cannot over stress this enough...*DO YOUR RESEARCH*!

You are in the business of helping others using your unique talents. But this is not about you. It is about those you help.

I have always loved the word "research". To me, the word means something new, exciting, and even fun. To others, when they hear that word, they think of something that is hard, tedious, and time consuming. If you relate with the latter, I challenge you to reframe how you view research.

Back when I was young, way before there was a thing called "the internet," research was done by taking a trip to the library, combing through pages and pages in encyclopedias and asking questions. Back then, research *WAS* a tedious, time-consuming task. With modern technology, all of this knowledge is literally at our fingertips.

When you are looking to create unique content, research is the key to standing out. Here's why:

- Research helps you know what's already out there. When you look into a topic, you can see what others have said before. This way, you don't just repeat the same old stuff. You can find new angles or ideas your competition has not talked about. Give the topic a fresh spin, throw in your unique views.

- Research makes your content more trustworthy. When you back up your ideas with facts and data, people are more likely to believe what you're saying. For example, you can use some statistics or facts to back up your content.

- Research also helps you understand your audience better. What are their challenges, struggles, pains and frustrations? How can you best help them? Are there tools or resources that you can identify that will help? By looking into what your audience cares about, you can create content that really speaks to them. You'll know what questions they have and the problems they want solved.

- Research can spark new ideas. As you dig into a topic, you might find connections or insights you never thought of before. This can help you create truly unique content that sets you apart.

Being seen as an expert is key to a successful business. Doing your research helps you build that expert status and stand out from the crowd.

One of my favorite tools (also listed in the *Useful Resources* section) is Perplexity. This AI tool was built for research. It offers access to current information. For example, if you're looking for statistics, Perplexity can find and sort multiple sources faster than you can by using traditional search tools. It is known for its accuracy and even cites the sources. This comes in really handy if you are not a research fan!

The Best Content Secret Ever

Repurposing content is a game-changer for coaches and consultants who want to grow their businesses without burning out.

Here's the deal: when you create a piece of content, like a blog post or video, you can break it down and use it in different ways. This saves you tons of time because you're not starting from scratch every time you need something new. For example, you could turn a long blog post into several social media posts, a video, or even part of an email newsletter.

But it's not just about saving time. Repurposing helps you reach more people too. Not everyone likes to read long articles. Some folks prefer watching videos or listening to podcasts. By presenting your ideas in different formats, you're making your content available to a wider audience.

Plus, when you share the same ideas in different ways, it helps your message stick. People often need to hear something multiple times before it really sinks in. It is said that it now takes 17 touch points before a prospect actually connects with you. So, by repurposing, you're helping your audience learn and remember your key points better. It also helps keep you in the front of their mind.

Another cool thing about repurposing is that it can show off your expertise in different ways. Maybe someone didn't quite get your idea from a blog post, but when they see it explained in a quick video, it clicks. This variety can help build trust with your audience and show them you really know your stuff.

Your time is precious. By repurposing content, you're working smarter, not harder. You're getting more value out of the work you've already done, which leaves you more time to focus on other important parts of your business, like working with clients or developing new offerings.

Keep That Engagement Going

I mentioned above that you need to measure and adjust your content accordingly. Let's expand on how you do that a bit further. Here's the thing. What works today may not work tomorrow. It is just the way the content world works. That awesome post you created yesterday may go viral, then a similar one, just a few days later, may fall flat and get zero engagement.

Does that mean it was bad content? No. People are fickle. One day they are all over fancy images and the next, a picture of your handwritten sticky note goes viral. This is why you need to make sure to monitor your content. You do this with content marketing analytics.

A MailChimp resource[18] describes content marketing analytics as follows:

> *"Content marketing analytics refers to the process of gathering and interpreting data related to content marketing efforts and using key performance indicators to measure the effectiveness of your campaigns. These analytics focus on measuring the performance of content across platforms and channels, from social media to your website.*
>
> *With content marketing insights, you can measure metrics like page views, organic traffic, engagement and conversion rate, social shares, and more. These KPIs can help you understand how your audience resonates and interacts with content, including which types of content are most successful and drives the most conversions to meet your particular objectives."*

The goal of monitoring your analytics is to make sure your content is working. For example, you may want to keep track of the number of reactions, comments and shares on social media posts. If you have a guide that users are downloading from a landing page, you'll want to track how many downloads you get. In your CRM, you'll want to see how many users are subscribing to your email list and how many are unsubscribing.

There are some easy-to-use tools out there to help track your content's performance:

1. GOOGLE ANALYTICS: It's free and shows you how people find and use your website.

2. META (FACEBOOK) INSIGHTS: Great for checking how your Facebook and Instagram posts are doing.

3. TWITTER ANALYTICS: See how your tweets are flying!

---

18   *https://mailchimp.com/resources/content-marketing-analytics*

4. LINKEDIN ANALYTICS: Helps you understand how your content is performing.

5. YOUR CRM: All CRMs have at minimum, basic analytic tools so you can keep track of who's opening your emails.

Different types of content have different things to track. At minimum, these are thing you want to monitor:

Social Media Posts:

- Likes, shares, and comments
- How many people saw your post
- Clicks on your links

Blogs:

- How many people read each post
- Which topics are most popular
- If readers click on other pages

Lead Magnets (like free guides or eBooks):

- How many people download or use them
- If they lead to more sales or sign-ups

Emails:

- How many people opened your email
- Who clicked on links inside
- Number of subscribers and unsubscribes

Videos:

- How many views you get
- How long people watch
- Comments and likes

Checking your analytics regularly is like giving your content a health check-up. It helps you make sure everything's growing strong and headed in the right direction.

Your Unicorn Factor

There you have it! We have demystified marketing content, and you have everything you need to set yourself apart from the crowd. It is time for you to take action!

By implementing what you have learned in this book, you will stand out and your business will grow as a result.

It is time to set your inner unicorn free. Here's to your success!

Useful Resources

There are literally thousands of resources available to help you with your marketing content. Here are a few of my personal favorites to get you started.

When picking apps to use, do your research. Ask others what they are using and get their feedback before you commit. Check out free trials when you can.

Analytics

1. GOOGLE ANALYTICS: (analytics.google.com) The gold standard for website analytics. Track your site's performance, user behavior, and conversion rates. It's a powerful, free tool that every marketer should master.

2. META BUSINESS SUITE: (business.facebook.com) Formerly Facebook Business Suite, this tool provides insights for your Facebook and Instagram accounts. Track engagement, reach, and audience demographics across both platforms in one place.

3. TWITTER ANALYTICS: (analytics.twitter.com) Get in-depth insights into your Twitter performance. Measure engagement, understand your audience, and see which tweets resonate most with your followers.

4. LINKEDIN ANALYTICS: (linkedin.com/business/marketing/analytics) For B2B marketers, LinkedIn's analytics tools offer valuable insights into your company page performance and audience engagement.

5. PINTEREST ANALYTICS: (analytics.pinterest.com) If your brand is active on Pinterest, use their analytics to understand which pins are driving traffic and engagement.

Content Creation Resources

1. ANSWERTHEPUBLIC: (answerthepublic.com) Uncover what people are asking online, a goldmine for content ideas.

2. COSCHEDULE'S HEADLINE ANALYZER: (coschedule.com/headline-analyzer) Craft headlines that grab attention and drive engagement.

3. CHATGPT: (chat.openai.com) An AI-powered writing assistant to help with ideation and content creation.

4. GEMINI: (gemini.google.com) Google's AI chatbot, great for research and generating content ideas.

5. CLAUDE.AI: (anthropic.com or chat.anthropic.com) An advanced AI assistant for content creation, analysis, and problem-solving.

6. PERPLEXITY: (perplexity.ai) An AI-powered search engine providing concise answers and citations, perfect for quick research.

7. FUTURETOOLS.IO: (futuretools.io) A comprehensive directory of AI tools for various marketing tasks.

Customer Relationship Management (CRM) Tools

1. MAILERLITE: (mailerlite.com) User-friendly email marketing with automation features.

2. MAILCHIMP: (mailchimp.com) A comprehensive marketing platform offering email, ads, and CRM tools.

3. KARTRA: (home.kartra.com) An all-in-one platform for online businesses, including marketing and sales funnels.

4. KAJABI: (kajabi.com) A Robust platform for creating and selling online courses and digital products.

5. ACTIVECAMPAIGN: (activecampaign.com) Advanced marketing automation and CRM with powerful segmentation features.

Design and Images

1. CANVA: (canva.com) A versatile platform for creating professional graphics without needing a design degree.

2. VISME: (visme.co) Create stunning visual content with this user-friendly tool. Great for infographics and presentations.

3. VISTA CREATE: (create.vista.com) Formerly Crello, this platform offers thousands of customizable templates to spark your creativity.

4. PIXABAY: (pixabay.com) A go-to source for free, high-quality images to enhance your marketing materials.

5. ADOBE STOCK: (stock.adobe.com) When you need that perfect, professional image and don't mind investing a bit.

Outsourcing

1. FIVERR: (fiverr.com) A global marketplace for freelance services across various categories.

2. UPWORK: (upwork.com) A platform connecting businesses with skilled freelancers worldwide.

Video Tools

1. VIMEO: (vimeo.com) A professional-grade video hosting and sharing platform.

2. DUBB: (dubb.com) A video communication platform designed for business engagement.

Webinar / Recording Apps

1. FACEBOOK LIVE: (facebook.com/formedia/solutions/facebook-live) A live streaming feature integrated into Facebook's platform.

2. ZOOM: (zoom.us) A popular video conferencing and webinar platform with robust features.

3. WEBINARJAM: (webinarjam.com) A comprehensive webinar platform tailored for marketing and sales presentations.

4. STREAMYARD: (streamyard.com) A live streaming studio for broadcasting to multiple social platforms simultaneously.

Recommended Reading

"The Conversion Equation" by Terri Levine

Learn how to create a steady stream of customers and profits.

"Hypnotic Writing" by Joe Vitale

Discover techniques to engage readers and boost sales through writing.

"Copywriting Secrets" by Jim Edwards

Master proven formulas for writing copy that converts.

"Blue Ocean Strategy" by W. Chan Kim & Renée Mauborgne

Explore strategies to create uncontested market space and outmaneuver the competition.

This toolkit covers a wide range of marketing needs. Whether you're looking to create eye-catching visuals, streamline your content creation, or manage customer relationships more effectively, these resources have got you covered. Happy marketing!

THE UNICORN FACTOR

Acknowledgments

"No one who achieves success does so without acknowledging the help of others. The wise and confident acknowledge this help with gratitude."

—Alfred North Whitehead

There are so many people who have supported me during this project.

I am honored to have Terri Levine write the Foreword for this book. I have been a client of Terri's for over four years, and it was at one of her mastermind events that *The Unicorn Factor* was born. I cannot thank her enough for her support and guidance as I have built this new chapter (no pun intended!) in my life.

And, who knew writing a book was going to be such a big project? Okay, in all honesty, I did, I just didn't know exactly how big of a project, especially for my first solo book. I had written chapters for a few other books, and they seemed pretty easy, basically because I wasn't doing any of the real leg work!

One of those books was called *Making Waves—Creating Ripple Effects That Can Change The World*. Again, Terri Levine was the driving force behind this book. It was in doing this project that I met Lil Barcaski, owner of GWN Publishing and the reason I actually finally finished my first solo publication.

Lil has the patience of a saint. I know because I challenged her patience every step of the way! She listened as I asked some of the silliest questions ever when it comes to publishing. After all, this process was all new to me! She even talked me off a couple ledges when I was seriously wondering if I was ever going to finish. I am eternally grateful for all her help and guidance. Lil and her amazing team at GWN Publishing are absolutely amazing.

To my husband and editor extraordinaire, Eddie. All my love for the hours of editing and listening to me think out loud about what was coming next and occasionally whining that this was a much bigger project than I ever imagined! You see, he has absolutely no clue about what I do in my business. This, and his solid knowledge of the English language and grammatical skills made him the perfect editor. Every time I gave him a set of pages to read, my first question to him was, "Did that make sense?" I figured if he could understand what I was teaching throughout the book, then I was on the right track. I really could not have done this without him.

For the many other friends and colleagues who knew I was working on this project who supported me 100% along the way; I am grateful to you all!

To you, my reader, thank you for taking the time to play along throughout this book. I wish you much success in your life and business.

About the Author

REGINA ANDLER is a Business Transformation Specialist who helps coaches and consultants attract more clients, guaranteed, through her proprietary methodology called The Unicorn Factor™.

For over 20 years, Regina has been an entrepreneur, successfully running a variety of businesses. She has experience with traditional brick-and-mortar businesses, online businesses, and multi-level marketing ventures.

Regina holds a Bachelor's Degree in Computer Science and an MBA. She is a Certified Jack Canfield Success Principles Trainer and is certified in Wholebeing Positive Psychology.

Before starting her own businesses, Regina worked her way up the corporate ladder in the tech world, from entry level to executive management positions.

Now, Regina uses her skills and experiences to help entrepreneurs build and scale successful businesses through her company, Autumn Ascent Consulting. She loves to share what she's learned to help others avoid the mistakes she made along the way.

In her free time, Regina enjoys being outdoors. She loves hiking, kayaking, playing golf, and participating in obstacle course races.

You can connect with Regina and learn more about her and her services at https://linktr.ee/reginaandler.

www.ingramcontent.com/pod-product-compliance
Lightning Source LLC
Chambersburg PA
CBHW071006120626
46546CB00003B/953